From
VICTORY
to
PEACE

From
VICTORY
to
PEACE

by

PAUL HUTCHINSON

The real problems of our generation are the problems
of victory, even more than the problems of war.

— *Owen Lattimore*

WILLETT, CLARK & COMPANY

CHICAGO   NEW YORK

1943

940.53
H97f

Copyright, 1943, by

PAUL HUTCHINSON

*All rights reserved, including
the right to reproduce this book
or portions thereof in any form.*

19931
April 1944

This book is manufactured under wartime conditions in conformity with
all government regulations controlling
the use of paper and other materials.

Third Printing

To
My friends of the
Alberta School of Religion
Camp Fairweather
near Calgary
July 1943

Preface

Behind the writing of this little book there are, in the main, two purposes. In the first place, it grows out of a fear that the governments are drifting toward a bad peace. Over against that I seek to present a sketch of the peace which the Christian church holds forth as alone containing the promise of a just and durable peace. In the second place, I hope to help some to understand that this peace which the church calls for is not something — in the expressive phrase of contemporary youth — "out of this world." I hope to show that it is realistic, attainable, required.

To achieve this second purpose I have resorted to a device, in the chapters devoted to the practical proposals of church bodies concerning the nature of the peace and the postwar order, which will soon become apparent to my readers. In every case I have tried to quote some secular source — some political leader who commands respect, some publicist, some magazine of standing — to show that there is impressive support from the "practical" world for the main positions taken by the Christian church.

We have been living for four years — really for twelve — in a world of war. We have thought war, planned war, waged war. It has been an exhausting and a humanly disintegrating business. Now it begins to look as though, in the not too distant future, we might have a chance for peace. Can we think peace, plan peace, *wage* peace?

It is a curious fact that we have little idea as to how the governments intend to go about this waging of peace. We think we know a little about Stalin's plans, but with the exception of a few generalities of doubtful application we know almost nothing about Roosevelt's and Churchill's. Yet the task of making peace and of establishing a stable postwar order seems to be committed almost wholly to the hands of these three men who, if they consult with anyone, do so in secrecy, while retaining all rights of decision in their own keeping.

I doubt whether this is a healthy state of affairs. All of us should be thinking about the peace and what is to follow. All of us should be discussing the issues at stake. All of us should be preparing to demand, and take, a share in the decisions. As peace nears, this discussion should fill every part of the democratic countries.

This book is an attempt to provoke such discussion. The positions which it supports are presented in as forthright and uncompromising a fashion as I have been able to contrive, first, because only clear proposals offer a solid basis for intelligent discussion, and second, because I believe that the church bodies which formulated most of these proposals were what my father used to call "everlastingly right." We need some right these days that is everlastingly right.

The difficulty of writing a book of this nature while events are so swiftly and continually changing the world picture needs no explanation. It may easily prove that there will be developments between the day when the manuscript leaves my hands and the day when it appears as a published book that will force changes in judgment on details of the world situation. But the underlying problems will not change, and the principles with which I have maintained that we should approach those problems are, I believe, permanently valid. Otherwise I would not have written.

August 31, 1943   P. H.

CONTENTS

APPENDIX

From
VICTORY
to
PEACE

CHAPTER I

WHEN JOHNNY COMES MARCHING HOME

I

It was around a campfire on the banks of the Bow river in western Alberta that I first heard it sung. The tune was familiar; any American school child can join in "When Johnny comes marching home." But these Canadians, with the intent purpose on their faces thrown into high relief by the flames from the blazing logs, had set new words to the old melody:

> When the boys come marching home again,
>   (By sea and air)
> They'll expect a hearty welcome then,
>   (Beware! Take care!)
> Democracy must find the way
> To peace and justice in a new day,
> So let's all build together in solidarity;
> Let's all build together for true community.

It was not the last time I was to hear that Canadian version of a song which has swelled from ten thousand military bands as men marched away to battle. The meter left something to be desired; even those who were familiar with the words betrayed a tendency to jumble syllables when they came to the line about peace and justice in a new day. But there was an insistence behind the words which could not be mistaken. Even now I can feel the ominous undertone of that warning: "When the boys come marching home again . . . beware! take care! "

To whom is the warning directed? To all of us who have stayed behind as ten million boys offered their lives to protect

us, our homes, our holdings, our institutions — all that we have
told them was threatened by a ruthless savagery. *We* sent
them out. We told them it was their duty to go, and in response to that mystic word they went — not enthusiastically,
not with much comprehension of the issues we said were at
stake, not with much anger at a foe or any lust for bloodshed.
They hated the whole dirty, brutal business. They resented
being thrust into it. Yet when we laid upon them the compulsion of that one word, ' duty,' they went. And now, in the
not so distant future, they are coming back again — those who
are left. They are coming back to face those who sent them
forth. They are coming back to us.

But they are not coming back as they went away. They left
us, most of them, boys. They will come back men. They are
men who have looked death in the face. They have borne
much, sacrificed much. Among them many have suffered
much. Some of them have been forced to pass through that
most shattering of human experiences — they have killed their
fellows, sometimes watching the death stroke fall which they
had inflicted, sometimes releasing from miles up the bombs
which they knew would blast the bodies of women and children in the crowded tenements of cities far below. And in the
empty hours of waiting — for all army life is filled with hours
of waiting — they have thought long, long thoughts. What
was this ' duty ' which swept them into such an inferno? Did
we who sent them to this horror, who laid upon them these revolting tasks — did we also have a ' duty ' to face and to perform? Have we faced it? Are we ready to perform it?

"When the boys come marching home again . . . beware!
take care! "

II

To no part of our Western society should the warning come
with more force than to the Christian church. For the Chris-

tian church, in its freedom to proclaim truth, presents itself as the principal custodian of many of the values which the soldiers of the democracies have been told they were fighting to preserve. The Christian church has made the great words so often invoked in wartime — words such as 'freedom' and 'right' and 'human worth' and 'sacrifice' — the familiar coins of its pulpit exchange. Even the concept of 'duty,' while no exclusive possession of the church, has been given much of its content and moral authority by the church. For every introspective, schooled mind who has gone into battle aware of the potency of the Kantian moral imperative, there have been a hundred thousand who have remembered most clearly, if they remembered anything, simple admonitions heard in some church nestled in the quiet countryside or in some Sunday school class in the roaring city, where they were first taught to believe that there is a *must* aspect of life which man evades at peril of his mortal soul.

> When duty whispers low, " Thou must,"
> The youth replies, " I can! "

Emerson said it in a way which spoke irresistibly to the American spirit, and ever since the pulpits of America have been echoing it, the schools and clubs and other instruments of the church have been graving it deep into the consciousness of young Americans. Now these same young Americans, having responded once again to the whisper of duty, are coming home, no longer young except in years, to confront the church with their insistent questions. To what end was this response to duty? Why all the killing and being killed? Why all the laying waste of human efforts? Why all the blighting of human hopes?

At no time has the Christian church found comfortable its relation to this war. When the war broke out, it did indeed believe that its coming was in large measure a condemnation visited upon the nations for their refusal to listen to the warnings of the church or to follow its prophetic teachings during the years of the Long Armistice. Yet that did not make it easier for the church to define its relation to the conflict, or make it ready to tell its sons what their individual response to the declaration of a national duty should be.

It is not the purpose of this book to trace the course of all the inner struggles which have beset the mind of the church while the war has pursued its bloody course. Suffice it to point out that even yet, as the war appears to be nearing its closing stages, there are commissions of theologians in Scotland and in the United States wrestling with the task of attempting to define the position which the Christian church, in the light of its gospel and its theology, should take regarding war. It is one more evidence of the power of the forces loosed among men by Jesus of Nazareth that the church which bows at his name has found this war an almost unendurable torture.

But no torment which has afflicted the church while the battle raged can equal that lying ahead. The years " when the boys come home," and immediately after, will be years to test the church as it never has been tested in modern times. They will be years when its faith will be tried to the uttermost, when its ministries will confront men whose great need is mocked by the greatness of their skepticism, when only a flaming evangel can attest its significance and competence to a generation which has been flayed until it has almost lost all capacity save the capacity to doubt and mock.

In one of the loftiest passages in classic Christian literature, St. Paul epitomized the characteristics of a Christian order. It would be one, he declared, in which the abiding values would be " faith, hope and love." Much discussion of the nature of a Christian postwar society has not changed that basic requirement. The churches may disagree among themselves as to the instrumentalities of world collaboration. They may disagree as to economic programs. They may disagree as to the future of empires. But on St. Paul's profound insight they must stand unitedly. The human order which they seek, which they preach, which they serve must keep alive and spread throughout the world faith, hope and love.

Yet these are the very elements most likely to be wanting "when the boys come marching home again." Victory will rest upon their banners, but doubt and dismay and resentment may gnaw at their hearts. In that prospect lies the sobering responsibility before the Christian church; its opportunity; its disaster if it fails to comprehend the requirement of the hour and measure up to it. At this point also arises the central question with which this book will attempt to deal. That question is: How may the Christian church keep alive faith, hope and love in a postwar generation threatened by a pervasive disillusionment and cynicism?

III

What sort of disillusionment lies in wait for the masses of men after the war?

For one thing, unless our political leadership discloses a capacity it has not so far revealed, our society is in danger of being swept by *the disillusionment of a bad peace*. It is frequently forecast that, following the present war, there will be no ' peace ' like that which closed the first World War at Paris in 1919, or like the formal treaties which have ended other wars in the past. This may well prove true. As this is written the possibility is growing that very soon Italy will agree to terms of surrender fixed by the United Nations, and that thereupon a separate peace of some sort will be arranged with the unhappy nation which Mussolini's folly plunged into the war. The Italian peace may be only a forerunner of a Hungarian peace, a Bulgarian peace, a Rumanian peace, a German peace, and at last a Japanese peace. If things work out in this fashion, there will then be no single peace conference, no one gathering to which the representatives of all the warring nations go to negotiate a single treaty or group of treaties ending the war.

But there will be agreements, even if entered upon one at a time with the different nations which have fought on the side of the Axis and even if negotiated over an extended period of months or years.[1] And these agreements will, in the common nomenclature, constitute the peace to end the second World War. Will that peace be good or bad? The signs are not propitious.

In saying this, one need not have in mind any perfectionist conceptions of what the peace should be. No peace treaty ever written was perfect in all its parts, and the peace treaties written by allies with conflicting or disparate interests are even more likely to contain undesirable compromises than those negotiated between single antagonists. That will be true again when the treaties are written which end this war. They will inevitably mirror the same pull-and-tug of competing national interests among the United Nations which operated at Paris after the first World War. Every thinking man anticipates this and has adjusted accordingly his hopes and expectations.

No, when one speaks of a ' good ' or ' bad ' peace one is thinking only in the rough-and-ready terms which are instantly un-

---

[1] It is possible, of course, that the process of disintegration in Europe may have gained such momentum by the time Hitler falls that the United Nations may find no way to write peace treaties with established governments in Germany and its satellite states. Revolutionary movements, such as swept Russia after the defeat of 1917, may turn an international war into a series of civil wars. This may be true not only in Axis countries, but in several of the now "occupied" countries which the Allies are pledged to restore. It is not difficult, for example, to see how some such chaotic internal struggle might follow the war in France. Should this prove to be the case, it will render largely beside the point the line of argument followed here, but it would increase the validity of the argument itself. Nothing would more surely provoke widespread disillusionment as to the worth of fighting the war than to have it succeeded by the spread of civil war, chaos and increased human insecurity across Europe and Asia.

derstood by the man in the street. According to these, a
'good' peace may be defined as one which secures at least a
semi-permanent stability in the world's political order and does
not obviously sow the seeds of future wars. And a 'bad' peace
may be defined as one which establishes no such stability, but
creates conditions out of which future wars are likely to arise.
Judged by these simple and reasonable standards — which are
the standards that will control the thinking of the masses of
men in the postwar period — there is every reason to warn the
Christian churches that they face the prospect of dealing with
a generation suffering from the disillusionment of a bad peace.

If this comes to pass, it will be the second such disillusionment to blight humanity within a quarter-century. Such tragic
disappointments of the human spirit are cumulative in their
effect. Especially will they cast a shadow over the relations of
embittered men with any institution which upholds the possibility of an order of faith, hope and love.

But why is it insisted that the prospects are now for a bad
peace?

Consider certain factors in the present situation. Consider,
for example, the refusal of the United Nations to announce
their peace aims. If ever there was a war in which a political
offensive based on a formulation of just, generous, hope-breed-
ing peace terms might have had devastating effect within the
ranks of peoples ground under tyrants, this would seem to be
such a war. The political offensive launched in 1917 on the
basis of President Wilson's Fourteen Points is conceded to
have played a major part in dissolving the war determination
of the peoples of the Central Powers. Yet no such offensive
has been launched in this war. Why?

Mr. Churchill made the reasons clear soon after assuming
office when, in denying calls from British liberals for a definitive
statement of peace aims, he frankly said that to publish such
aims would threaten the internal unity of England. To win

a war, national unity at home is a prerequisite. Once let the
nature of the postwar arrangements envisaged by the sort of
government which Mr. Churchill heads be published, and large
portions of the British public would find themselves at logger-
heads as to the wisdom and worth of the ends sought.

The same consideration doubtless inspired President Roosevelt, as late as midsummer of 1943, with the Axis front already
beginning to crumble, to admonish the American people that
" this is not the time to engage in international discussion of
all the terms of peace and all the details of the future. We must
not relax our pressure on the enemy by taking time out to
define every boundary and settle every political controversy in
every part of the world." As that veteran publicist, Oswald
Garrison Villard, pointedly remarked, " telling the Germans
and Italians just what will happen to them is not taking time out
for nothing, but for a momentous step toward the enemy's
collapse." Yet this step, incessantly and almost unanimously
demanded by liberal opinion in the United States and Britain,
has not been taken.

Now there is a certain short-range political canniness about
this refusal to formulate publicly peace aims with regard to
Europe or Asia which should be acknowledged. But there
are ominous implications as well. If such aims cannot be announced while the war is in progress, because to do so would
be to introduce irreconcilable divisions into the home front,
then it follows that our national leaders expect the peace itself
to prove a source of disappointment and a cause of criticism
among important portions of the populace. And from that
logical deduction it is only a short step to the fear that one reason why the United Nations have refused to tell what they
intend to do with the peace — as, for illustration, in the case of
the former European colonies now occupied by Japan — is that
they dare not do so lest they weaken their own ostensible unity
or raise questions among the soldiers as to the worth of the

ends for which they are chancing death. Would China approve the peace aims which Mr. Churchill and Mr. Roosevelt have for Hongkong, Indo-China, Malaya, Burma, Java, Sumatra or Borneo? Would Russia? Would the American boy facing death in the fever-infested jungles of New Guinea? Would the American mother who wonders whether he will ever come home again?

Or consider the indications of the political record which the United Nations have made in the war so far. What kind of peace is forecast by our ' expedient ' dealings in North Africa? It is still too early to bring in a final verdict on the Darlan episode. As with so many other events shrouded by secrecy during war, we cannot hope to know even the approximate truth about this one until all the " Now It Can Be Told " books and all the memoirs of the participants have appeared ten, twenty or thirty years after the war — when our knowledge will be too late to do us any good. But this much is plain to any eye, that in the subsequent struggle between Giraud and De Gaulle we have become involved in a controversy between two French leaders, one owing his position entirely to our support, and the other owing his rapidly growing popularity among the French people largely to the fact that we are understood to oppose him. Does such a record hold forth much promise of adequate wisdom for dealing with other competing leaders and parties in regions whose political problems are infinitely more unfamiliar and incomprehensible than those of France?

In this same connection one must not overlook the strange maneuvers in which the American and British governments have become involved with figures as ill-omened as Otto of Hapsburg, Tibor Eckhardt, Otto Strasser and even Hitler's former intimate, " Putzi " Hanfstaengl. While so much remains in the realm of surmise, there is nothing to be gained by speculating on the reasons why adventurers of this stripe should have been so cordially received in high quarters while tried and tested democratic leaders, self-exiled from the various fascist terrors of Europe, have found the atmosphere of the State Department at Washington and of the Foreign Office at London distinctly chilly. But the British publicist, Professor Harold J. Laski, knew whereof he spoke when not long ago he addressed an open letter to his friend, President Roosevelt, asserting that liberals in England are alarmed by the friendliness shown for Franco and the King of Italy and the most conservative elements in prewar France. Said Mr. Laski:

Mr. Hull may be angry when these curious relations are criticized by his press conference; he perhaps regards it as a challenge to his good faith. We are, on the contrary, certain that Mr. Hull has all the best possible intentions. But we sometimes suspect that the streamlined power-diplomacy of Mr. Berle and Mr. Dunn, the heroic embodiment by Mr. Robert Murphy of the sophisticated role of a Ruritanian diplomat, the shrewd hints (in the best Massachusetts tradition of John Adams) that Mr. Ray Atherton not seldom reveals of the need to make the new world one that is run by the old men for old purposes, are all of them indices to an attitude of mind which may easily result in old Metternich being the one man whose ideas have a permanent place at the peace conference. We refuse to believe that the pinchbeck Metternichs of Washington have the right to speak to Europe, still less to lay their plans for its reorganization, in your name.[2]

Nor is the political record with respect to disputed territories more reassuring. At the moment, there appears to be complete disagreement between the Russian and Polish governments regarding the disposition of former Polish territory after the war. Russia demands what diplomatic language calls " rectification of military frontiers," as a means of widening the moat between the Soviet Union and western Europe. The Polish government-in-exile, remembering that Britain ostensibly entered the war to fulfill her pledge to maintain the terri-

[2] From the *New Statesman and Nation* of London, April 10, 1943.

torial integrity of Poland, is insisting that in the event of victory the United Nations must restore the Polish frontiers as
they existed before the war. Russia declares that the regions
which she occupied while still an ally of Hitler must remain,
for security reasons, in her hands. Great Britain and the
United States, accordingly, are reduced to the unimpressive
role of bringing to bear what pressure they can on the Poles
to induce them not to force the issue with the Russians while
the war continues. Rumors circulate that the Poles are being
asked to agree to Russian annexation of eastern Poland with
a promise that they can obtain compensation from the annexation of East Prussia. Whatever the outcome of such a dispute,
it patently will leave in eastern Europe an area of thwarted
ambitions, national anger and continuous tension — a festering
source of intrigue and future trouble.

A few months ago the United States and Great Britain announced, with the self-satisfied air of powers who had committed an act of unprecedented generosity and abnegation, that
they were about to abrogate the 'unequal treaties' with their
ally, China. The abrogation failed to impress the Orient,
which knew that the extraterritorial rights thus surrendered
had been given up by other nations — as, for instance, by Russia
and Germany — decades ago, and that they were rights which
no Americans or Britons in China had been able actually to
exercise for years past. The gesture of generosity, in other
words, was largely empty. But at the same time, the Chinese
government informed the British of its desire, as part of the
postwar settlement, to review the position of Hongkong, the
British crown colony taken from China as part of the spoils of
the Opium Wars. Since Hongkong is at present in Japanese
hands, its disposition after the Japanese have been driven out
would naturally seem to be subject to consideration in the
peace treaties. However, the British government brusquely
informed China that it would not allow the question of any re-

turn of Hongkong to Chinese sovereignty to be raised. China could hardly carry the issue further at that juncture because of the war requirements for ostensible unity among the United Nations. But if anyone believes that, after the war, China will be satisfied to see this great city and port, which has controlled the economic life of south China, returned to European hands, or will permanently accept such a decision, he must be extraordinarily ignorant of the currents now sweeping through the political life of the Far East.

All these incidents, already arising out of the political developments of the war, are little more than episodes in such a period of global confusion. Taken together, however, they tell a story, they forecast a prospect, which can hardly be mistaken. One need not be an alarmist to conclude that they reveal among the nations which will be victorious no more magnanimity of purpose, no more imaginative wisdom, no more readiness to seek to enter a new era in world affairs than the victorious nations disclosed in 1919.

Or consider, again, the likelihood for a bad peace inherent in the very difficulties of peace-making. Here is a problem which, as every reader will know, could be developed for pages. I prefer simply to suggest its nature by asking a few questions.

If peace should break out tomorrow, and if you — the reader — were given absolute power to fix the nature of the peace terms, what provisions would you decree in order to insure the future prosperity, security and political stability of France? What provisions would you impose on postwar Germany in order to make the eighty million Teutons a bulwark of European peace rather than a constant menace to world order? What would be the peace provisions you would put into effect for the Balkans, bearing in mind on the one hand the insistent need for some sort of federated economic life in that trouble-breeding region and on the other Soviet Russia's fear of feder-

ations on her frontiers as possible links in a chain of encircle-
ment? In the service of lasting peace in the Near East, what
would you do about Palestine? Or in the Far East, how would
you deal with the problem of the future of Japan's seventy million people — they will not starve in silence — while liquidat-
ing the illicit ambitions of Japanese imperialism?

These are samples of the political problems with which
the peace must deal. A dozen others might be cited, almost
equally difficult. There is hardly a government-in-exile, for
example, but represents such a problem. Then there are the
economic problems of the coming peace, which are equally inescapable and equally difficult. What, for instance, would
you, as the architect of peace, do about Germany's economic
future? Would you repress the German technological and industrial potential, or would you encourage its development?

To one who ponders such considerations, the evidence that
this war will be followed by a bad peace will not be conclu-
sive. Nevertheless, the *danger* of such a peace must be apparent, and its likelihood must be admitted to be very great. If
there is a bad peace, what will be the effect on people buried
under astronomical national debts, their sons and husbands
killed or so maimed as to face years of frustration, with little
prospect ahead except back-breaking taxes and endless international tensions? The effect, it is safe to predict, will be seen
in a society shot through and through with disillusionment.

IV

What sort of disillusionment lies in wait for us after the war?
Consider the prospect for *the disillusionment created by a continuing social crisis.*

In 1919, at the very time John Maynard Keynes was uttering
his doleful — and, as it was to prove, all too well justified —
prophecies in his *Economic Consequences of the Peace,* the
Lloyd George government fought and won a general election

in Britain largely on the slogan, " A land fit for heroes." Much the same hope and expectation is being instilled in the popular mind today. The period of the war has been, perforce, a period of belt-tightening and sacrifice. But the peace, it is believed, is to usher in a day of plenty and of economic security. Has not President Roosevelt declared that the war is being fought to assure the Four Freedoms, not in " a distant millennium," but as " a kind of world attainable in our own time and generation "? Has he not said that the one freedom basic to all the others is " freedom from want "? And has not Vice-President Wallace promised that " the peace must mean a better standard of living for the common man, not merely in the United States and England, but also in India, Russia, China and Latin America — not merely in the United Nations, but also in Germany and Italy and Japan "?

But is that the way it is to be? Not to concern ourselves for the moment with the prospects for postwar " freedom from want " in India, Russia, China, Latin America, Germany, Italy or Japan, but to fix our attention on the American industrial scene as it is today, what do we see? The typical business tycoon, the man who has spent ten exasperated years cursing " that man " in the White House, today goes about in a glow of anticipation that the day of his deliverance is at hand. Even the probability of " that man's " re-election for still another term fails to dampen his expectations seriously, since he believes that the executive, after the 1944 election, will be held in leash by a conservative Congress which can be trusted to permit no more economic or social nonsense. If the expectations of big business could be fully known, I believe that hope of a return to normalcy in the best Harding-Mellon tradition, minus the cruder lootings of another Ohio gang, would be disclosed.

And the big businessman has ample cause to sit back and lick his chops with anticipatory gusto. Already he sees the farm vote, wooed and rewarded during the years of the Roosevelt administration as never before, flocking back into the Republican column. He sees the conservative wing of organized labor, at last given dynamic leadership by a John L. Lewis whose Roosevelt-phobia knows no bounds, preparing to support almost any Republican candidate. He sees the bourbonism of the South, frustrated at the polls, finding compensation in the support of one reactionary proposal after another on the floor of Congress.

The very catchwords of an economy of abundance, so often heard two or three years ago, have fallen into disrepute. ' Planning ' is no longer a hope for the future; ' planning ' has become a synonym for ' regimentation ' and an agent for the proliferation of ' bureaucracy.' When the President submits to Congress the modest proposals of the National Resources Planning Board for extension of social services to guard against a postwar return to mass unemployment and social insecurity, those proposals are promptly thrown into a committee pigeonhole and Congress displays its real temper by voting the NRPB itself out of existence.

Henry Wallace, the vice-president of the United States, who persists in talking as though an economy of abundance were a realizable prospect, finds himself being swiftly relegated to the ranks of the crackpots, with most of the inner circle of the administration assisting.

Nor is the prospect brighter in Great Britain. Despite the façade of a national government, Britain actually is more firmly in Tory hands today than it was under Neville Chamberlain. The treatment accorded the Beveridge plan should make that plain. The Beveridge plan (*R.I.P. 1943*) constituted no threat to capitalism. The only vested interest it could be construed as threatening in any important degree was that of the private insurance companies, and these had only to render a genuine service at a reasonable cost to maintain their position. Sir William Beveridge proposed nothing more than an extension of familiar plans of social insurance to Britain's entire population, at a tax cost remarkably low. Yet the Beveridge plan was greeted as ' revolution ' — " Moscow come to London " — and reposes now in some parliamentary mortuary with all too little prospect of a postwar resurrection.

So little hope does the Labor party hold out to wrest power from Tory control that the appearance of the Common Wealth party, led by Sir Richard Acland, has been generally interpreted as a last desperate resort of younger Englishmen to find some postwar alternative to Tory policy short of violent revolution. The Common Wealth platform differs only slightly from traditional social democratic proposals, seasoned with a touch of evangelical fervor. It stems directly from the famous " Acland amendment " adopted by the Malvern Conference of Anglican churchmen in 1941. (More of Malvern later.) Yet so deeply entrenched is Tory power in England, and so determined to maintain its privileges, that sober observers of the life of the tight little isle declare that any attempt to put into effect the property nationalization planks in the Common Wealth platform would almost certainly involve England in a major constitutional crisis which might not stop short of civil war. If that is true with regard to the proposals of Sir Richard Acland and his followers, what would happen if the British Communist party should knock at the gates of power? [3]

Here and there optimistic voices suggest that drastic economic and social changes can be expected after the veterans of

[3] Another indication of the unyielding and untempered nature of Tory class control in England was provided in the defeat administered this year to the exceedingly mild proposals for reform of working conditions in the catering trade, as contained in a bill introduced into Parliament by Ernest Bevin. Yet Mr. Bevin, a member of the Churchill cabinet, is supposed to be one labor leader whose influence with the masses is so great that Conservatives in Parliament might have been expected to go to great lengths to satisfy his wishes as a means of keeping war production at its peak. Mr. Bevin knows better now.

the war return to take their part in national affairs. These men, who are supposed to have been reflecting on the inequities of the present order during their months in the service, will, it is predicted, demand social reforms of a sweeping nature when they come home to face more insecurity in the labor market with continued inequalities in the distribution of the national income. They will demand that the socialism of the firing line be transferred to the home front.

How much basis of likelihood is there for such a forecast? One fears, very little. I write, of course, as one outside the army, who cannot claim first-hand knowledge of what the soldiers and sailors are thinking about the future. But such information as I can gather points in the direction of an intention to form veterans' associations whose principal purpose will be to operate as pressure groups in securing special privileges for those with service records.

The veterans may know little about a Beveridge or an NRPB report, but they *all* know, at least vaguely, of the successful raids on the federal treasury made by the G.A.R. in the four decades following the Civil War, and they *all* know, extensively, of the way in which the American Legion and other organizations of veterans of the first World War mobilized political power to secure preferential positions in the public service, adjusted compensations and bonuses, and to set the stage for a vast pension scheme which will presently provide a lifetime federal income for all men who were in any way connected with the fighting forces during the former war. With ten million men under arms in this conflict, what more natural than that they should expect to extract benefits from the public purse on a scale never hitherto approached?

Since unplanned economies find themselves increasingly subject to the manipulations of pressure groups, it is as safe a postwar prediction as can be made that, before demobilization is completed, the manufacturers' lobby and the farmers' lobby and the labor lobby and the cattle growers' lobby and the cotton lobby and the silver lobby and all the other lobbies will find their inexhaustible appetites for government handouts dwarfed by the demands of the veterans' lobby. In an order largely made up of a patchwork of special privileges and grants to special interests able to control blocs of votes, what else is to be expected? If anyone is to be granted special advantages at the hands of government, who has a better claim than the man who has risked his life in the national defense?

President Roosevelt has already indicated the shape of things to come by his promise of demobilization payments to discharged soldiers and sailors on a scale never before known. His opponents have denounced this as an effort to win the soldier vote in the election of 1944, but the only way in which they can counter is by promising to pay out more. It is not only the election of 1944, but every election until 1976 which is on the auction block.

Moreover, such evidence as is now obtainable suggests that the veterans will return to their homes filled with resentment against much of the population, especially factory labor, which they believe has been profiteering at the soldier's expense while he has been daring the dangers of battle. Poorly informed, or even seriously misinformed, as to the causes of work stoppages and strikes in war plants and mines, these veterans may prove in no mood to seek anything in the way of economic adjustment save new forms of "adjusted compensation" which, it will be claimed, will make up for the inflated income of the war years gained by farmers, factory workers and the others who stayed at home.

It is not my purpose here to enter into any discussion of the rights and wrongs of this prospect. But it must be pointed out that any such employment of the veterans' unquestionable political strength will work powerfully to throw the national economy out of balance. It will make it necessary to continue indefinitely deficit financing of the government, thus increasing rather than cutting down the enormous national debt which will have piled up by the close of the war. Continue this for a few years and the hopelessness of the outlook will drive the country toward one, or many, of the possible forms of repudiation which will leave the veterans — along with all the rest of us — with government IOU's in their hands and economic disillusionment and bitterness in their hearts. Remember what happened to the morale of the French people who, after winning what they were told was a glorious victory, were subjected to Poincaré's 80 per cent devaluation of the franc!

Still one other aspect of the economic outlook deserves mention. Is there any guarantee that the economic disaster which followed the first World War will not be paralleled after this conflict? On the contrary, are not all the elements present for an even greater disaster?

After World War I, it will be remembered, capitalism plunged into a period of profit-taking which persuaded many of its champions that the day of permanent prosperity had arrived. Consumers' goods were rushed into the vacuum created by the belt-tightening of the war years. Innumerable foreign loans, supposedly paying high rates of interest, were floated on the American market, where a bond-buying public had been created by the educational processes of the Liberty loan drives. Some of these were intended to repair war ravages, some to pay Germany's war indemnities, and some simply to line the pockets of South American politicians who must have laughed at the gullibility of North American investors while they marveled at the irresponsibility of the banks and investment firms which foisted such ' securities ' on the market. Agriculture, to be sure, began to suffer deflation from the day of the armistice, and went from bad to worse until the New Deal launched its general economic salvage operations.

It took only ten years for the bubble of postwar prosperity

to blow up to its fullest size and then burst. In Europe, of course, it never blew to any size at all, as those can testify who remember the tragic textile towns of Lancashire and mining towns of Wales, the bitter poverty of Germany, the baffled anger of the demobilized French peasants, the near-chaos which gave Mussolini to Italy. But in the United States the bubble grew . . . until suddenly foreign bonds began to tumble en masse into default, the market for consumers' goods began to sag, the first jittery employers began to cut wage scales, and before most of us could comprehend what was happening a cycle of economic contraction had been set in motion which presently had veterans selling apples on street corners and Wall Street financiers diving from skyscraper windows.

Have we learned enough to prevent this from happening again? Will there be no more attempts to impose unpayable reparations at the close of this war, no more demands to " squeeze them till the pips squeak "? Will there be no rush to exploit a market starved for consumers' goods, along with a madhouse scramble to get for nothing the fifteen and a half billion dollars' worth of new industrial plants built by the government during the war, and a flying leap into the something-for-nothing excesses of installment buying? [4] Will the inevitable sag in employment, certain to imperil twenty million workers in war industries while plants are being retooled for peacetime production, bring no corresponding effort to take advantage of a glutted labor market by cutting wage scales? Let the reader answer.

It is possible that such forebodings may, in the event, prove unwarranted. It is possible that, by drastic taxation and a

[4] If an effort is made to hedge against the dangers of an installment consumers' market by urging the conversion of war bonds into consumers' goods — as much of the advertising being done by large American firms now forecasts — that very conversion, if on a large scale, may do more to shake the structure of government finance than any other action could.

policy of economic planning daringly conceived and rigorously applied, the full employment of the war years may be succeeded by the full employment of an economy of abundance based on production for maximum consumption rather than production for private profit. Yes, that is possible — and the possibility is directly related to the functioning of the social conscience of the churches in a way presently to be discussed. But if that does not come to pass, then we must expect to see great masses whose faith and hope in the economic future has given place to disillusionment and despair.

v

Or, finally, consider the prospect for holding aloft the ideals of faith, hope and love when confronted by *the disillusionment of the returning soldier.*

This is so distasteful a subject that little more will be said about it than to point to its existence. But the churches, in particular, have little conception of the gravity of their postwar task if they do not realize that, in so far as their relations with the men who return from the front are concerned, they must deal with millions of men suffering from deep and lasting psychic wounds.

During every great war cheerful souls go about chattering of the soldiers' return to religion. It does not matter that wars are almost invariably followed by periods of moral letdown; even the high idealism which helped to sustain both sides in America's civil conflict could not protect the nation from the slimy corruption of the succeeding Gilded Age. There are, we are assured, no atheists in foxholes — a claim which apparently leaves out of account a good many heroic Russians. And every tale of a Rickenbacker saved by a sea gull, or of a soldier whose pocket Testament has stopped a bullet, is seized on by these prophets of a religious revival as evidence that the soldiers will come home proclaiming that the hand of the Lord was in it all and that it is their purpose henceforth to laud and magnify his holy name.

Somehow, it never works out that way. Soldiers return taciturn, introspective, impatient of any attempt to involve them in discussion of the experiences through which they have passed. (I am talking now of those who have actually been in action, and of the years when they are fresh from the battle-line.) Civilians find hard to understand, and sometimes resent, this characteristic reticence of the true veteran.

There should be no mystery about it. These are the men *we* have sent out to suffer terrible things and — far worse in so far as the psychic result is concerned — to inflict horrible suffering on others. They have done these things "in line of duty," but it was a duty for which they had no stomach when they performed it and which revolts them when they think back upon it. I could cite instances, but I will not. The appalling fact is that there will hardly be a reader of this book but who, if he knows a front-line soldier intimately, will presently see evidence of these psychic wounds bared before his eyes.

And what will be the actual attitude of these returning soldiers toward the church? In the case of some of them (let us hope many of them) all other considerations will be overborne by the personal contacts which they have made while in service with wise and courageous chaplains. For the rest, however, there will be questions which no personal relationships, however warm, can down. Why should they have been called on to do these brutal, these altogether revolting things? What boy who has seen the effect of a block-buster bomb on a Naples tenement, or has carried out orders for the "summary disposal" of a malaria-riddled Japanese on Guadalcanal, can survive that act without coming to loathe not simply the act itself, or himself as its doer, but the society which involved him in the necessity of doing it, and the institutions of that society?

Let the Christian church never think that it can escape this questioning. It is one of the institutions which have claimed a right to survival. Many of its leaders, individually and in group manifestoes, have asserted that its future, its opportunity to preach a full gospel, was inextricably bound up with the defeat of the enemy. If it has not proclaimed a holy war — and to the church's eternal credit be it said that it has not this time — it has raised no disclaimer when nationalistic propaganda has pointed to the church as chief among the values which the warriors fight to preserve. But when a church presumably committed to the service of faith, hope and love allows men, without protest, because of a necessity which it cannot gainsay, to participate in the ghastly acts which modern war involves, how can it expect these men to come back from hell without a deep questioning — yes, skepticism — as to the reality and relevance of that church's gospel?

How many Christian hymns, one wonders, make sense to a soldier who has cleared a dugout with a hand grenade or to an airman who has machine-gunned a boat filled with helpless troops escaping from a sinking transport?

VI

These are some of the reasons, but only some, why it is said that the postwar problem of the Christian church — as of all the institutions of society — is the problem of maintaining the possibility of an order permeated by faith, hope and love in the face of a pervasive disillusionment. Never will the need for this Christian vision of a human order be greater than on the day when the firing stops. Never will its attainment seem more impossible; never will its proclamation seem more absurd. Can this presage for the churches anything but a future of increasing impotence, a time when their ministries will be regarded with indifference and their preaching with contempt?

It is the contention of this book that no such fate need overtake the Christian church in the postwar world. That it is in danger of such a fate even this hurried survey of the probable nature of that world should make plain. But these pages are being written in the profound conviction that, if the Christian church recovers and discharges its prophetic function in relation to man's search for a better order, the very disillusionments produced by the war and by the failure of secular processes will serve to make men newly conscious of the church as the custodian of an eternal wisdom. Accordingly, it is to consideration of the requirements of this prophetic function that the remainder of this book is devoted.

CHAPTER II

MORAL LAW AND THE VOICE OF PROPHECY

I

Confronted alike by the fumbling of governments which have found no way out of the morass of power politics and by the imminence of a wave of popular disillusionment, another period has dawned when the Christian church must raise again the voice of prophecy. But how can the church be sure that it speaks a true prophetic word, the veritable word of the Lord to a dismayed and skeptical generation? How can it be sure that the policies and courses for which it claims its highest sanctions will not prove, when tested by time, to have been folly? Historically, the line between the prophet and the fanatic has been very thin. The scriptural admonition, "Test the prophets," had generations of experience behind it.

What distinguishes the true prophet from the irresponsible visionary? It is his possession of a stable basis of faith, of firm standards by which to measure his own judgments, of criteria for men's actions which apply under all conditions and for all time. Lacking these, the prophetic impulse soars away into vagary or, bruised by the rebuffs of human indifference or rejection, sinks into the mere mouthings of a liturgical pretense. But possessing these, the prophet can maintain a true objectivity toward his time — which is the essence of prophecy — judging men's shifting deeds and stratagems in the light of principles which do not themselves shift.

Has the Christian church, for this particular emergency, such dependable standards of reference on which to base its prophetic judgments? The Delaware Conference, held by American churchmen three months after the United States entered the war, declared that it has. As this book grows largely out of a belief that the Delaware Conference represented the closest approximation to competent discharge of prophetic responsibility by any important section of church leadership since the outbreak of the war, the declaration of that body that the Christian church has an undeviating and immutable set of standards by which to judge the acts of the nations in forming the postwar world, is of the utmost importance. This affirmation will be found implicit in the first and second of the thirteen " Guiding Principles " which the Delaware Conference laid down as preface to all its detailed pronouncements concerning political, economic and social aspects of the problem of winning a just and lasting peace.

The Delaware Conference contended that it is the present responsibility of the Christian church to judge the peace proposals and postwar policies of the nations on the basis of the moral law. There is a whole charter for Christian prophecy in the uncompromising terms in which the conference put forward these two basic declarations:

1

We believe that moral law, no less than physical law, undergirds our world. There is a moral order which is fundamental and eternal, and which is relevant to the corporate life of men and the ordering of human society. If mankind is to escape chaos and recurrent war, social and political institutions must be brought into conformity with this moral order.

2

We believe that the sickness and suffering which afflict our present society are proof of indifference to, as well as direct violation of, the moral law. All share in responsibility for the present evils. There is none who does not need forgiveness. A mood of genuine penitence is therefore demanded of us — individuals and nations alike.

This, it scarcely needs to be said, is not the language in which nations discuss the issues of war and peace. Neither does it provide a religious sanction for their practices. On the contrary, it stands in condemnation of those practices. For the international practice of nations is based on expediency. It follows the path of self-interest. Its patron is Machiavelli, not Moses. Its law is not the moral law, but the law of survival, the law of the jungle, the law which is in truth no law, but anarchy.

When the nations make appeal to the moral law, it is as a propaganda device to fasten opprobrium on their enemies. Defiance of the moral law is something that my enemy does to defeat me. What I do to defeat him is simply that which national interest requires, and which military necessity accordingly justifies.

When the Christian church, sweeping aside or ignoring all such rationalizations, takes its stand on the integrity and authority of the moral law, it has an impregnable position from which to pronounce prophetic judgment. Its concern is then with what, in the light of its perception of the moral order, should be. And because of its faith in this moral order, it can demand that what should be, shall be. It need not, and it will not, be bounded in its expectations by what the secular mind declares is possible or practicable. To a prophetic church, that which accords with the moral law is possible, and only that which accords with the moral law is practicable. " The excellent becomes the permanent " — and *only* the excellent.

Here is salvation for both society and the church, if we will but see it. There is salvation for society in building for the long future and according to principles which compel the assent of all men of probity in all lands. The damnation of our social order, the damnation which again lies in wait when peace-making time comes, results from our enthrallment to the short perspective, our readiness to adopt the seemingly expedient which always seeks to cloak some deviation from justice. And there is likewise salvation for the church which, unless it thus discharges its prophetic office, grows ethically insensitive, dull to human values, oblivious of long-time consequences, and presently finds itself on the road to disaster.

To such churchmen as may shrink from the penalties which an unrepentant society will try to inflict upon a church that attempts thus to speak with the voice of prophecy, history provides stern reminders. Even during the present generation, in the fate which it visited upon the church of tsarist Russia history has afforded a new warning of what happens to a church when it neglects or evades its prophetic function.

II

Perhaps the healthiest thing which has recently happened within the Christian church has been the renewed assertion of the reality and authority of the moral law. Here, in the realm of its ethical responsibility, the church had been well-nigh ruined by the delusions of relativity. Einstein's word, seized on as a former generation seized on catchwords from Darwin, had almost destroyed man's belief in any moral stability. Morality, it was held, is no more than a reflection of social customs and tabus (the *mores*); as society changes its moral standards will change with it. Thus the ' right ' becomes something different to each generation, each culture. And the ethical demands of religion are to be accorded respect only within narrow limitations of time and place. Conduct is good or bad *relatively speaking*.

It should hardly be cause for wonder that a generation inoculated with this virus should presently find itself wallowing in such moral excesses as have turned the world into a madhouse. The flippancy of a Reno-bound scoffer at the sanctity of the home has been of a piece with the sadistic brutalities of the Berlin scoffers at the sanctity of human personality. Only the

scale of such moral nihilism has differed.   Never has there
been an ethical perversion so sure to bait mankind's oldest and
most destructive moral trap — " the end justifies the means."
The whole sorry record of these recent years which the locust
has eaten, these years upon which men everywhere look back
with disgust, could be written in terms of the effort to make
this ancient casuistry, " the end justifies the means," the ethical
basis for society.

Delaware's " Guiding Principles " show the church shaking
off this paralyzing mood of moral relativism.   "Moral law undergirds our world."   The " moral order is fundamental and
eternal."   " Social and political institutions must be brought
into conformity with this moral order."   The evils which afflict
society " are proof of indifference to, as well as direct violation of, the moral law."   There is tonic in the mere reading
of such declarations.   Here is none of that apologetic " Well,
perhaps, under certain circumstances . . ." tentativeness
which has emasculated so much of the church's moral teaching
since the days of Herbert Spencer.   Rather, here can be heard
once more some of the thunder of Sinai.   It is high time that
men should hear again from Sinai.

When the church talks thus about a fundamental and eternal
moral order and a moral law operating within that order, what
does it have in mind?   It has in mind its conviction that there
are certain imperatives which are common to the experience
of all men with full faculties, and that there is a certain order,
an order of community, which men of insight in all times and
under all circumstances regard as the goal of human desire and
effort, the only fit order for man.   It is not for me, who can
pretend to no competence as a moral philosopher, to attempt
an exact statement of this moral law or description of this
moral order within which it functions.   But even the tyro can
distinguish the main landmarks on this landscape.

First of all, the church believes that there is a quality of *oughtness* (Kant called it a moral imperative) about our lives which lies beyond the reach of choices. We do not stand in doubt; we simply know that there are certain things we *ought* to do. We may not do them; our tragedies come from the fact that we do not do them. But when we do not, we know that we have betrayed something basic within ourselves as creatures of Nature. What have we betrayed? We have betrayed our sense of the need to be loyal to our highest ideals. And to the extent of our betrayal we have made ourselves unfit to live with ourselves. Only the man whose mind is sub-standard can betray his highest ideals and not suffer in his own estimation.

But this sense of *oughtness* demands more than loyalty to oneself. There must be loyalty to others as the basis for community, for no community of hypocrites and double-dealers can long endure. There must be concern for others; otherwise men will mutually destroy one another, and no society can exist. There must be regard for the pledged word; even among savages experience has taught that without this society will fall to pieces. There must be acknowledgment that possession, position and power impose obligation; call it *noblesse oblige* or St. Paul's principle of the responsibility of the strong for the weak or what you will, but the recognition of such obligation is to be found from the moment man begins to form society. And there must be the effort to do justice, to hold the balances evenly, to do to others as you would have them do to you. Without the sense of a principle of justice operating between men, social order cannot survive.

This is the working of moral law, for it enjoins that pattern of conduct which experience and reason have everywhere and always convinced reflective men must be observed if man is to live at peace with himself in society. And man cannot live at peace with himself out of society. Robinson Crusoe was bound for madness until he discovered Friday's footprints.

III

On the basis of the moral law, accordingly, a prophetic church may take up its task of subjecting society to analysis and criticism. In discharging such a function it will have no concern with the expediencies which pass as political realism. Its sole responsibility is to proclaim what should be; it is content to believe that its Lord, who is the Lord of history, will see to it that what should be eventually becomes what must be and then what is. But its present duty, as a prophetic voice, is to see that men have placed before them, so clearly that they cannot remain in ignorance, knowledge of what should be, in the light of the moral law. In relation to such public issues as are involved in making the peace and forming the postwar order, the Christian church has no other responsibility than the discharge of this prophetic task.

On five occasions since the outbreak of the war important groups of church leaders in Great Britain and the United States have attempted to outline the nature of peace terms and of a postwar society to which the Christian church could give its approval. The first of these came on December 21, 1940, when the four ranking churchmen of Britain — the Anglican Archbishops of Canterbury and York, the Roman Catholic Archbishop of Westminster and the Moderator of the Free Church Federal Council — put forward joint proposals for the consideration of statesmen after the war. There were ten of these proposals.[1] The first five had been formulated by these English clerics. They were concerned with the nature of a society capable of enduring and living at peace. The second five proposals, however, had originally been put forward by Pope Pius XII in a speech delivered by the pontiff a year earlier, on December 24, 1939. The English statement may therefore be

---

[1] The text of this document, and of all the principal documents adopted by the bodies mentioned in this chapter, will be found in the Appendix.

regarded as an amalgam of the views of the leaders of Roman Catholicism, Anglicanism and British non-conformity as these were held a little more than a year after the outbreak of the war.

Of much greater importance were the deliverances of the conference of Anglicans which convened at Malvern College, England, from January 7 to 10, 1941. Presided over by Dr. William Temple, then Archbishop of York and now Archbishop of Canterbury, this conference included 23 bishops, 14 deans, 125 other clergy and about 70 lay members of the Church of England. It proceeded on the assumption that a just and lasting peace for the world requires the existence of a just and lasting society within the dominant nations; that the inequities of society are a result of " loss of conviction concerning the reality and character of God and the true nature and destiny of man," and hence that the problem of peace is basically a problem of religious evangelism. Of the many forms in which the Malvern Conference sought to frame this evangel, none was more striking than its call for radical reorganization of the economic and administrative life of the Church of England, and its adoption of the " Acland amendment," with its characterization of private ownership of " the great resources of our community " as " a stumbling-block " which makes it " harder for the generality of men to live Christian lives," and its demand for an order of society from which this stumbling-block is removed. Only those who remember the days when the Church of England was described as " the Tory party at its prayers " can appreciate the historic significance of a conference of this sort, held by Anglicans and presided over by the Primate of England.

A little more than a year later, from March 3 to 5, 1942, almost 400 delegates from 27 American communions met at Delaware, Ohio, in a National Study Conference on the Churches and a Just and Durable Peace. The conference was convened by the special commission, under the chairmanship of Mr. John Foster Dulles, which the Federal Council of the Churches of Christ in America had created fifteen months earlier to consider that particular question. It contained clerical and lay delegates, a few of the latter seemingly gravely concerned lest its views of economic and social issues give aid and comfort to radical forces in American life. No body convened in the United States since Pearl Harbor has been so well equipped to reflect the thinking on peace issues of a cross section of the non-Romanist churches. To a remarkable degree, as further chapters of this book will attempt to make clear, the Delaware Conference measured up to its responsibility and opportunity.

Not so much is known about the origins of the fourth declaration from church sources on the nature of the peace. On March 18, 1943, almost exactly a year after Delaware, the Federal Council's Commission to Study the Bases of a Just and Durable Peace suddenly presented to the public " A Statement of Political Propositions " which, because it was drawn in the form of six brief theses, has become popularly known as the " Six Pillars of Peace." These theses were first unveiled at a dinner held in a large New York hotel. They quickly received approval from such newspapers as the London *Times* and the *New York Times*. They have been widely circulated through the press, and have been approvingly commented on in print by leading diplomatic and political figures.

Finally, there met at Princeton, New Jersey, from July 8 to 12 of this year, 61 church leaders from 12 different countries, including citizens and former citizens of countries with which the United Nations are at war. This conference also was convened by the Federal Council's commission, in collaboration with the Commission on Church, Nation and World Order of the United Church of Canada. More government officials and persons holding intimate relations with heads of government war agencies attended the Princeton Conference than had been present at any gathering under church auspices since the outbreak of the war. The conference avowed three purposes: " (1) To obtain further information on issues wherein the application of Christian principles and of political propositions derived therefrom involves peculiar difficulties and complexities; (2) to promote better understanding of the views held by Christians in different countries; (3) to formulate, in so far as possible, a consensus of views on the problems of order in the postwar world." Acting as individuals, the members of the conference adopted *A Christian Message on World Order* and *A Message to Christians Separated by the Barriers of War.*

Other formulations with regard to the war, the peace and the nature of the postwar order have been drawn up by other Christian bodies, on the Continent as well as in England and America. To attempt, however, to review all these would be to smother such a book as this under a mass of documentary material. And it is not necessary. By keeping steadily in view the pronouncements in these five documents, it is possible to judge to what extent the Christian church has prophetic insight into the needs of men and nations today.

I believe that the church has disclosed far more such prophetic insight in the Ten Principles of the British leaders, in the Malvern Manifesto, in the Delaware Findings, in the Six Pillars and in the Princeton Message than a bewildered society yet comprehends. Even the rank-and-file membership of the Christian communions has yet to learn in any detail the content of these historic documents, to say nothing of grasping their implications. And the task of making these formulations known to the leadership of the nations and to the public at large has scarcely been begun. Yet the day when collapse of the fascist forces will bring the obligation to begin postwar rebuilding is almost at hand. The prophetic voice of the church must be sounded abroad very soon — or the hour of opportunity will pass forever.

" On the basic moral principles of justice and the love of one's neighbor as oneself," declared the Princeton Conference, " the church must call for consideration of (1) the extent to which each state should accept the establishment of an international authority responsible for the maintenance of law and order among the nations and for limiting the independent national control of armed forces; (2) the extent to which each state should limit the independent ordering of its economic life in such matters as tariffs, import quotas and currency, with a view to promoting the common welfare of mankind; (3) the government of one people by another (as in the case of colonies or defeated nations) and the degree of international control required to insure that such government, where it exists, shall be used for the purpose of preparing the way for equality; (4) how race prejudice may be overcome, equal dignity and opportunity accorded to all races, and justice secured to religious and racial minorities."

With the task thus defined, and the basis of the church's judgment made clear, let us turn to consideration of the principles of action for which the church stands and must stand.

CHAPTER III

The Search for a World Community

I

During the Long Armistice a thoughtful British publicist, G. Lowes Dickinson, wrote one of the most penetrating studies ever made of the causes of our modern global wars. He entitled it *The International Anarchy*. Its basic contention was compressed into that title. The clash of national ambitions and interests continually leads to war, Mr. Dickinson made clear, because there is no true sense of world community, because every nation insists upon exercising unrestricted national sovereignty. Unrestricted national sovereignty involves, for every nation, the claim to be judge of its own interests and disputes and to act without control from any outside party. In other words, it is international anarchy.

Here lies the crux of the problem of world peace. In disputes between individuals, there is common agreement that no man should be the judge of his own cause. All the processes of dispensing justice in organized societies rest on this principle of bringing in some disinterested third party to decide between the disputants. But the claim to unrestricted national sovereignty, when made in the relations of nations, denies this same principle in the international community. Consequently, there can be no true international community.

When a nation begins to talk about its sovereignty, to insist that nothing must be allowed to infringe upon its sovereignty, what it really means is that, because it claims independence, it claims the right to do as it pleases. If it is not left entirely free to do as it pleases, it will not be entirely independent.

But just as no man can be entirely independent while living in an ordered community, so no state can be entirely independent in a world order which is other than anarchy. That is why the *Economist* of London, perhaps the world's leading economic journal, has said that "the absolute sovereignty of the state, operating on two different planes — the national and the international — has wrought more havoc in the recent life of man than any other single principle." Today the fundamental problem in seeking a just and lasting peace lies in recognizing the fact of the interdependence of nations and seeking means by which to organize this fact in suitable international institutions. The 'patriot' who persists in keeping the flag of unrestricted national sovereignty flying above his land is simply casting his vote for a continuation of world anarchy and endless war.

To say this is not to deny the great contributions which nationalism has made to modern life. There is some danger lest, in our indignation against the anarchic tendencies of the nationalistic spirit when carried to excess, we fail to give proper credit to the values which nationalism has created or enhanced. Not everything which flowed out of the break-up of the Holy Roman Empire or the rise of the Renaissance was loss. Human energies have been released, human devotion has found noble means of expression, human freedom itself has been extended by the nationalistic urge. There are still resources of human will-power inherent in nationalism which should be neither suppressed nor ignored. Are we, for example, to regard the stirrings of the nationalistic spirit in China or in India or in Java or in Turkey as something to be deplored?

Nevertheless, the time has come when, for the sake of world peace and in the name of the moral law, the principle of absolute national sovereignty must be challenged. It must be challenged because this principle has been elevated in recent years to the status of a religion in some nations, and from this religion have sprung those evil seeds from which have sprouted fascism and state totalitarianism. Edward Shillito, the British writer, placed his finger on the core of our trouble when he wrote the book which he entitled, *Nationalism — Man's Other Religion*. For this " other religion " has too often proved stronger, has too often been more intensely held and practiced, than the traditional faith to which man gave formal adherence.

H. G. Wells in one of his books portrays in striking fashion the way in which modern man has come to give primary devotion to his nationalistic tribal gods. My recollection is that the passage occurs in the *Outline of History*, but a hurried search through the many pages of that monumental volume has failed to discover it. However, I recall its nature clearly enough. Mr. Wells contrasts what might have happened to a traveler crossing Europe by stage in, say, the sixteenth century with what might happen to a traveler crossing in a railway compartment today. Had the sixteenth century traveler spoken slightingly of the doctrine of the Trinity or of the mystery of the Nicean formula as to the nature of Christ he would quickly have found himself in serious difficulties. He might even, as did Servetus in Calvin's Geneva, have found himself at the stake. But today the traveler might indulge as he pleased in theological speculations, yet if he spoke disparagingly of John Bull or La Belle France or the Stars and Stripes or Germania — or of any of the other symbols of national pride — he would be headed straight for trouble. Nationalism has become " man's other religion."

But even nationalism is not an insurmountable obstacle on the road to peace unless and until it is linked with the claim to unrestricted sovereignty. In actual practice, as we all know, unrestricted sovereignty can be exercised only by great powers. Small states, whatever their claims to independence, must shape their policies to conform with those of their powerful neighbors, or suffer distressing consequences. Thus, in the decade before the outbreak of the present war, a state like Yugoslavia discovered that she had no recourse but to accept a fifteen years' supply of aspirin as 'payment' for the copper and wheat demanded by Germany, Greece had perforce to accept tons of mouth organs as 'payment' for her tobacco and raisins, while Bulgaria had to accept a million cameras without lenses as 'payment' for the tobacco and meat that the Nazi economy demanded. When the United States adopted a tariff which dealt a body blow to Czechoslovakia's shoe and glass industry, what could the Czechs do about it?

The heart of our problem in seeking a world community, in other words, lies with the few great powers which can attempt to maintain an actual absolute sovereignty. But even these can pursue a course of unconditioned self-interest only at a terrific cost. Their refusal to pool their interests with the interests of others involves the maintenance of enormous forces, for they must know that if their interests come into conflict with those of others then the others will, if sufficiently antagonized, form combinations of power for the counter-assertion of their own demands. Maintenance of unrestricted sovereignty by any power is, therefore, a short-term policy which is certain in the long run to involve that power in trouble and to contribute to the spread of international anarchy.

The moral should be plain. It appears immediately when the precepts of moral law are applied to the affairs of the nations. World peace is thus seen to be dependent, first of all, on the achievement of world community. And world community waits until the most powerful states recognize their obligation to seek the welfare of others as well as their own. "*And the second is like unto it, Thou shalt love thy neighbor as thyself.*"

II

Has the Christian church prophetic insight clear enough to deal with this problem of attaining a world community? It has.

In the fourth of its " Guiding Principles " for the establishment of a just and durable peace, the Delaware Conference spoke this clear, prophetic word: " We believe that the principle of cooperation and mutual concern, implicit in the moral order and essential to a just and durable peace, calls for a true community of nations. The interdependent life of nations must be ordered by agencies having the duty and the power to promote and safeguard the general welfare of all peoples. Only thus can wrongs be righted and justice and security be achieved. A world of irresponsible, competing and unrestrained national sovereignties, whether acting alone or in alliance or in coalition, is a world of international anarchy. It must make place for a higher and more inclusive authority."

Every word in this declaration carries tremendous meaning, for almost every word is a challenge to the practice and intentions of the great powers and to the thinking and emotional bent of the majority of their peoples. But, lest these words be dismissed as no more than general aspirations, not to be expected to have an immediate effect on the policies of the victorious nations at the close of the war, the Delaware Conference followed them with two sections of specific proposals, written in its committee on the political bases of the peace and adopted by the conference as a whole:

That certain powers now exercised by national governments must, therefore, be delegated to international government, organized and acting in accordance with a world system of law. Among the powers so delegated must be the power of final judgment in controversies between nations, the maintenance and use of armed forces except for preservation of domestic order, and the regulation of international trade and population movements among nations.

That international authorities competent to perform these functions may be of two sorts. (1) The ultimate requirement is a duly constituted world government of delegated powers: an international legislative body, an international court with adequate jurisdiction, international administrative bodies with necessary powers, and adequate international police forces and provision for world-wide economic sanctions. (2) As steps toward, and potential organs of, such world government, there is need for many sorts of international bodies charged with specific duties, such as the International Labor Organization, and various agencies such as those now acting for the United Nations to coordinate natural resources, shipping and food distribution. Such bodies must be adapted to the service of world order and government, and must not become a substitute therefor. In the operation of these agencies, and in progressing toward full world government, every effort should be made to achieve agreement and the voluntary cooperation of all concerned.

We need not stop at this point to discuss all the specific proposals contained in these declarations. But the nature of the world order here envisaged, as demanded by this body of Christian churchmen with unhesitating emphasis upon that unbending word, "must," cannot be mistaken. *In the name of the Christian church, and on the basis of what is "implicit in the moral order," there is here demanded a world community of nations, owing allegiance to a true international law, defined and administered by international agencies, with those prerogatives of national sovereignty so far surrendered that all nations give over the right to final judgment in their controversies with other states, the right to set the size and control the use of their armed forces, the right to fix the basis of international trade and population movements!*

If it be said that this is a conception of a world order utterly beyond attainment at this time, if it be objected that no great power in the flush of victory would so much as consider this diminution of its sovereign authority, then the answer of a prophetic church must be that it is not concerned to define the politically expedient; it is concerned only to set forth, in the light of its comprehension of moral law, the nature of a world community in which, because justice reigns, peace will endure. If man, with his institutions, refuses to make the adjustments required by this prophetic ideal, then man must suffer the consequences. The responsibility of the church has been discharged.

Seemingly, there were those within the ranks of church leadership who, once the nature and implications of the Delaware declaration sank in, drew back from this prophetic pronouncement. Did it require too much? Did it expose the church to the charge, from secular quarters, of an impossible idealism?

In the year which followed the Delaware Conference a slow attrition of men's hopes for the nature of the postwar order undoubtedly set in. Men talked less and less of an inclusive community of nations, with the sovereign powers of the great victors circumscribed by methods of cooperative action. They talked more and more of a combination of conquering states, imposing its will upon the defeated and upon all those nations with restricted military and economic strength. Finally, on March 21, 1943, the British Prime Minister and war leader broadcast his expectation for the future. It took the form of a Council of Europe — to be paralleled by a Council for Asia and, one infers, a Council for the Americas — " a council of great states and groups of [weaker] states," a council not much different in composition and intent from that born a hundred and thirty years ago in the Congress of Vienna.

Perhaps it is not to be wondered at that church leaders, sensing this regression in the secular mind regarding the nature of the postwar world, should have sought to meet it by a similar regression in their own thinking. There is a lamentable difference between the declarations of the 1942 Delaware Conference, which have been quoted, and the first of the 1943 " Pillars of Peace " which the church Commission to Study the Bases of a Just and Durable Peace made public only four days before Mr. Churchill's historic broadcast: " The peace must provide the political framework for a continuing collaboration of the United Nations and, in due course, of enemy and neutral nations."

What was there here to which any politician on the winning side, however narrow in his nationalistic outlook, would not agree? What was there here which differed, in spirit or in purpose, from all the ancient devices of power politics by which the nations have fruitlessly sought to control the earth and escape war in the past? With what devastating effectiveness had the feeble attempt to wrest some saving concession from this proposal for a Grand Alliance been emasculated by the insertion of those weasel words, " in due course "!

Fortunately for the prophetic integrity of the church, this feeble essay in power politics has not been allowed to stand as the word of the church concerning the search for a world community. Four months after the appearance of the Six Pillars, delegates from North America, Europe, Asia, Australia and New Zealand gathered in Princeton, New Jersey, to study the effects of the war on the world-wide interests of Christianity and to plan for postwar reconstruction. Was it the influence of Christians from the weaker nations — the Netherlands, Switzerland, China, Japan, Canada, Australia, New Zealand, Germany — which brought forth a declaration repudiating the concept of a victors' alliance and going back to the sound insight of Delaware? Or had the American and British delegates themselves grown dissatisfied with the temporizing and timid position of the first of the Six Pillars?

In any event, Princeton now revived the prophetic accents
of Delaware when, in a statement outlining " Requirements for
Progress toward World Order," it said:

Progress toward our goal will require:
1. That national isolationism, the monopolization of political
power by a few nations and the balance of power, which hitherto
have failed to maintain peace, be repudiated as policies which contravene the purpose of establishing world order and the institutions requisite thereto.
2. That temporary collaboration among the United Nations
should, as quickly as possible, give way to a universal order and
not be consolidated into a closed military alliance to establish a
preponderance or a concert of power. . . .
4. That immediate international collaboration such as is involved in (a) conferences dealing with specific problems and in
(b) the administration of relief and reconstruction be guarded
against exploitation for purposes of power politics.
5. That if regional organizations arise, they shall be part of an
inclusive world order and shall not threaten the interests of world
organization.

Such a concept of the requirements of world community
and order is a salutary rebuke to a short-range vision bound
by the adventitious alliances of the present war. It has nothing in common with Mr. Walter Lippmann's proposed postwar alliance of the " arsenal nations " — Russia, Great Britain
and the United States — even though it appeared at the very
time when American magazines and newspapers were ringing
with cheers for that proposal. It stands unwaveringly for a
" world-wide political order " as " for us an imperative obligation inherent in the Christian world view." In this Princeton
declaration can be felt once more the authentic pulse of Christian prophecy.

Nevertheless, while Princeton represented ground regained
from the retreat in the Six Pillars, it did not, one must regret-

fully admit, take the church all the way back to the clear light in which it stood at Delaware. For the Princeton declaration is indecisive on the basic problem of the necessary abrogation of unlimited national sovereignty if a just world order is to be obtained, and it is silent — ominously silent — on the pressing issue of the early freedom of subject peoples. Because of these silences and ambiguities, the statement sent out from Delaware remains that to which bewildered men should look when seeking to discover the best leadership which the Christian church has to offer for the crucial years that lie just ahead.

III

In the Delaware declaration, then, we find the clearest portrayal of the sort of world community which the Christian church holds can maintain a just and durable order of peace. It is to be " a true community of nations," including within its purview the interests of " all peoples." Ultimately it is to take form in " a duly constituted world government of delegated powers," with appropriate legislative, judicial and executive branches, together with " adequate international police forces." As immediate means toward this ultimate goal, international bodies with specific responsibility for the discharge of inescapable tasks of world rehabilitation and coordination are envisaged. But these interim agencies are not to be allowed to become substitutes for the ultimate, inclusive international body. The goal of the " duly constituted world government " is always to be kept in view.

What nations are to have a part in the tasks of this " true community of nations "? All nations! There is to be no distinction between victors, vanquished and neutrals. For the emergency steps to be taken immediately after the firing stops, " during a transitional period " when perhaps only interim commissions can function, Delaware called for participation by " the efforts of the peoples of the world." In none of its proposals for short-term or long-range action did it make any distinction; the basis of the " true community " is always inclusive.

At Princeton there was, indeed, an attempt made to draw a line. Apparently believing that it would be difficult to find a way by which the defeated nations, if not the neutrals, could be immediately brought into the work of succor and preliminary restoration which must immediately follow the " Cease firing " order, the Princeton churchmen specified that " temporary collaboration among the United Nations should, as quickly as possible, give way to a universal order." The decisive words, of course, are " as quickly as possible." How quickly is " as quickly as possible "?

Without wishing at this juncture to deal with the whole subject of disarmament (for which see Chapter VII), I believe that " as quickly as possible " means as soon as the fascist nations have been disarmed. From the moment of their disarmament their capacity to disrupt or destroy the efforts of the other nations to build a peaceful world order will disappear. From that moment, also, failure to include them in the tasks of world rehabilitation will feed the same national neuroses which contributed so greatly to the tragedy which followed the first World War.

But in saying this, it must be borne in mind that disarmament should, in the view of the church, be multilateral. " For one or more nations to be forcibly deprived of their arms," said Delaware, " while other nations retain the right of maintaining or expanding their military establishments, can only produce an uneasy peace for a limited period." But if disarmament is to be general, it will have to be immediate. Otherwise, as Herbert Hoover has demonstrated, and as happened in connection with the vague promise of disarmament made by the Allies in the Treaty of Versailles, disarmament will never take place at all.

Very well then, we have the conception of an all-inclusive

body of disarmed nations working to establish a " true community of nations." How should this all but impossible task be undertaken? As to this, also, Delaware had guidance to offer. Instead of following the example of some church bodies which, having outlined ultimate goals, when means are mentioned take refuge in the phrase, " We leave that to the experts," Delaware at least sketched the sort of means which it believed could be successfully employed. What were they?

In the first place, it laid down the principle, as already stated, of general participation in immediate works of mercy and restoration. The relevant passage in the Delaware report, which occurs in the section on the political bases of a lasting peace, will repay careful reading:

That during a transitional period after the fighting has ended, the efforts of the peoples of the world be devoted, in proportion to their ability, to the re-establishment of order, the provision of food, shelter and medical service, and the restoration of stable government and economic activity, especially in the devastated territories. These emergency measures must include policing by joint action for the protection of minorities and disarmed populations, and positive measures of economic and cultural cooperation. They should be carried out under international authorities, representative of all peoples concerned. There should be no punitive reparations, no humiliating decrees of war guilt, and no arbitrary dismemberment of nations. All of these emergency measures should tend toward a growing structure of international order.

The idea here is essentially that which will be found in many of the books in which secular students of the problem of postwar integration of the nations have made their proposals. For example, in *The Economic Consequences of the Second World War*, Lewis L. Lorwin of the Brookings Institution (hardly a source of visionary sentimentality or idealistic vagaries) outlines five independent international organizations which he believes should begin to function to block the advance of chaos and to lay the foundations for a new world order immediately after the end of the fighting. Dr. Lorwin's commissions would include an International Relief and Social Assistance Commission, a World Economic Development Organization, an International Colonial Administration, a Permanent Peace Conference and a World Educational and Recreational Center. Overarching all these he proposes the establishment of a World Assembly of Nations which, while having only powers of recommendation to the five functioning bodies, would meet annually to review reports and make suggestions to them.

It is Dr. Lorwin's belief that this sort of operating entity, placed in action as an emergency measure to deal with the near-chaos which will exist at the close of the war, would gradually develop into a true world federation of nations. But it would avoid initial debates regarding the extent of the surrenders of sovereignty required from participating nations; the necessity for action would come before everything else; only in action would the nature of the needed limitations on sovereignty be determined. The close resemblance between the plan proposed by Dr. Lorwin and that envisaged in the Delaware recommendation is obvious.

Other American proposals to get a postwar world order functioning by means of emergency international commissions, thus leaving the consideration of the theoretical issue of national sovereignty until there is actual machinery for world cooperation in being, have been brought forward from many quarters. The suggestion of this sort made by former President Herbert Hoover and former Ambassador Hugh Gibson, in *The Problems of Lasting Peace*, is especially notable because of the weight of experience behind it. Equally thought-provoking, as coming from a British source, is the plan outlined by Professor Edward Hallet Carr, in his *Conditions of Peace*, for four international economic bodies to go to work in Europe the minute the war ends. These would include a relief commission to care for the casualties of the war, a transport corporation to get the railroads and other communications operating again across boundary lines, a reconstruction and public-works corporation to keep peacetime economic processes operating on the same scale as have the wartime industries, with all these heading up in a general European planning authority, empowered to work out a cooperative and coordinated economic program for the entire continent.

However, the crowning proof that the Delaware proposals are not simply dreams of visionaries who have no contact with reality is to be found in the growing evidence that they closely approximate the very measures which the United Nations plan to take. So far two conferences have been held by the United Nations to lay the groundwork for postwar action. One of these considered the problem of refugees; the other the problem of feeding. As a result of this second conference, a United Nations' Relief and Rehabilitation Convention has been drawn by the American State Department which would establish an international commission to combat starvation and begin the work of international reconstruction immediately after hostilities cease. This convention is now the subject of negotiation among the United Nations, as well as between the State Department and the foreign relations committee of the United States Senate. If it goes into effect — as, with some modifications, it seems certain to — it is understood that it will be followed by still other agreements, growing out of later conferences of the United Nations, covering still other phases of the gigantic task of rehabilitation which will confront the nations after the war.

In other words, the general nature of the plans which the United Nations are making to start an international postwar cooperative program functioning, and the proposals toward this end approved by the churches at the Delaware Conference, are in agreement.

IV

There is, however, a word of caution which the churches have spoken at this point. These interim commissions which are to start the wheels of international cooperation turning at the close of the war must not, as Princeton warned, " be consolidated into a closed military alliance to establish a preponderance of power or a concert of power." That is to say, they must not be so completely organized by, administered by, staffed by and directed by any Big Three or Big Four of the victor nations that, as their operations gradually lead toward and develop into a permanent method of international action, a world control by alliance of military powers will come into being.

That this is a real danger inherent in the plans now under consideration in Washington and London (and presumably in Moscow) has been made plain by the protest already addressed to the American State Department by the Dutch government regarding certain features of the Relief and Rehabilitation Convention. This protest points out that " the composition of the central committee is not in accord with democratic principles " — which is a diplomatic way of saying that the control of food distribution under the convention would, in the plan as presented, be concentrated in the hands of the United States, Great Britain and Russia, with China exerting some influence on the program in Asia. Since, in a period of threatened starvation, food control is equivalent to political and economic control, the government of the Netherlands has taken its stand against allowing such enormous power to be assumed by the Big Three. In making its protest, it is understood, the Dutch government has simply acted as the voice of other small nations ostensibly included in the total of thirty-three United Nations.

At stake here is an issue whose importance cannot be minimized. If the distribution of food by an international commission after the war is made subject to the complete control of three powers, then a precedent will be established out of which will develop, almost inevitably, that very consolidation into a concert of power attempting world control against which church leaders have warned. Behind the protest against the present nature of the Relief and Rehabilitation Convention made by the Dutch lies the whole question of the nature of the postwar order. Is it to be a voluntary, cooperative and growing community of nations, or is it to be a military alliance? Is it to be inclusive, giving the small nations their due part in contributing to the welfare of the whole? Or is it to be a closed body of " arsenal " powers — to use Mr. Lippmann's term again — which gives orders to the rest of mankind, demanding obedience or else . . . ?

At this point, also, the question of future relations with enemy nations deserves consideration. Much has been said about the necessity for re-education of the fascist nations if they are to become capable of peaceful cooperation in a world community. Most of this discussion has been in terms of the re-education of Germany, a matter to which Vice-President Wallace has directed public attention on several occasions. But everything said about the necessity of re-educating German youth, after years of exposure to the false doctrines of fascist philosophy, applies equally to the youth of Italy and Japan. Unless the minds of the rising generation in Axis countries can be reached and changed, German, Italian and Japanese youth in 1960 will prove as susceptible to the cult of force and ruthless pursuit of power for its own sake as did the youth of those nations during the years which led up to the tragedy of 1939. All who think deeply on the problem of establishing a durable peace will agree that this re-education of Axis youth lies close to the center of that problem.

But how is genuine re-education to be carried through?

Many Americans and Britons, and even certain educational bodies in the two countries, apparently think that the problem is simply one of reorganizing schools and curricula. Let there be a postwar international commission for the control of schools; let there be international commissioners appointed to administer or supervise the schools in Axis countries; let internationally certified schoolmen go through textbooks with fine-tooth combs, carefully eliminating fascist ideas and substituting democratic doctrine. Then let the international commissioners see that teachers, following these purged textbooks, teach only sound history, sound economics, sound sociology, sound politics. The result, it seems to be expected, will presently be a generation of young Germans, young Italians and young Japanese bubbling over with democratic enthusiasm and indistinguishable in their loyalties from young Americans, young Britishers or young Russians.

It would be hard to contrive a more fatuous mess of nonsense. Leaving out of account the fact that it would almost certainly be impossible to obtain agreement between the United States and Britain on one side and Russia on the other as to what constitutes sound history, economics, sociology and politics (a consideration in itself sufficient to preclude any such policy of re-education), it should be said that any person who will support this as a method for actually changing the mental outlook of fascist youth knows nothing of history and less of human nature. Modern history is studded with the utter failure of just such attempts. Every power which carved up Poland tried, by rigid supervision of schools, to make young Poles into Russians or Prussians or Austrians. All they succeeded in doing was to make them into fanatical, chauvinistic Poles. Much the same thing happened in Ireland and in Alsace-Lorraine. Much the same thing has happened in Korea. Education of this type, enforced at the bayonet's point, simply makes the proliferation of underground methods of instruction (frequently directed by priests and pastors) a patriotic duty for the old and a glorious patriotic adventure for the young. It will inevitably and completely defeat its own ends.

No, the only re-education of Germany (or of its allies) which will be worth anything to postwar peace will be of a sort which the Germans seek for themselves, participate in willingly and find personal satisfaction in seeing carried to success. Where is such re-education to be sought? It should be sought by enlisting Axis youth after the war in full-fledged cooperative participation in all the tasks of rehabilitation and new development which will confront the world. It should be sought by opening opportunities for service under just such international commissions as are now being projected, thus making all such international action inclusively cooperative from the earliest possible moment.

Axis youth will return from the fighting fronts bitter, disillusioned, more than a little shell-shocked, apprehensive. A policy of re-education which is essentially punitive will drive toward sullenness, despair, festering hate, the determination to seek revenge. But a policy which offers opportunity to participate in world enterprises will open the eyes of young Germans, young Italians, young Japanese to the possibility of a different and more rewarding future than ever Hitler or his like held out.

The sort of re-education which might conceivably change the mind of the new generation in Axis lands would say to these young people, " Come, here's a gigantic task to be done. An entire continent is to be rehabilitated. A whole world's industrial order is to be set back to functioning. There is tremendous salvage and reconstruction work to be done all over the globe, as well as in your own shattered land. Let us attack these tasks together." Here would be an approach positive in spirit, psychologically sound, and Christian in motive. The re-education would come in the cooperative doing.

Faced by such an opportunity, the neuroses of fascism would begin to fade out of the minds of Germans, Italians and Japanese. No longer would the youth in what has been an Axis country feel himself either a pariah or an Ishmaelite. He would have no reason to sulk, to nurse imagined wrongs, to plot, to nurture that evil spirit of desperation and irresponsibility which had hitherto made him a Nazi, a Fascist or a Nipponese chauvinist. He would enter a new mental atmosphere. When the Axis mind has thus been changed, the world would have no further reason to fear the curriculum of the schools. The German people, the Italians and the Japanese would themselves look after that.

V

The goal before the nations, therefore, is an inclusive world community, in which absolute national sovereignties shall be substantially modified to make place for cooperative international controls. As Delaware phrased it: " The problem confronting the world is how to substitute for the idea of self-preservation of the individual state the primary importance of the society of nations, and the principle that the good of the whole takes precedence over the good of the part, since the highest and ultimate good of the part is itself so largely conditioned by the good of the whole." When the ideal held aloft by the Christian church is realized, there will be a world government with delegated powers, organized and acting in accordance with a world system of law, claiming from all men a world loyalty which transcends, while it does not supersede, all national and local loyalties.

But while this goal is clear to the prophetic eye of the church, and must be kept by the church clearly in view before all men, it cannot be achieved at a bound. The road toward it will prove long and rough. The immediately important requirement at the close of the fighting, it follows, is that the nations shall be induced to enter on the first stages of that road. What are those first stages? They seem fairly clear.

First of all, as has already been stated, there must be general participation in liquidation of the war, the war method and the war spirit by disarmament. At the same time, as has also been shown, there must be general participation in the work of succor and rehabilitation through emergency commissions. Beyond this, however, the steps to be taken will of necessity depend on the response of the peoples and the conditions created by the initial procedures.

As means toward the progressive diminution of unrestricted sovereignties, resort may be taken to the development of regional associations (but bearing in mind the Princeton warning that " they be part of an inclusive world organization and shall not threaten the interests of world organization "), to the negotiation of special agreements to free and speed trade between nations on the general order of the American trade pacts, or to the building of a genuine and recognized body of international law by means of the decisions of a revived World Court.

All these possibilities lie too far in the future and are too dependent on intervening developments to make it necessary to treat them in detail. The main requirement is simply that progress be started and kept moving in this general direction. For this is the direction in which, after they have had sufficient experience in cooperative action, the nations will come at length to the place where they will be willing to constitute a World Federation with affirmative powers. From there the road to the world government for which a prophetic church has called runs straight and plain.

VI

It seems wise at this point to refer briefly to the subject of policing. Almost every treatment of the problem of establishing a world community calls for policing in some form. It is held that, just as the local communities with which men have been familiar have required police protection against lawless elements, so any world community will require the presence of some form of police force. The Delaware report is specific in demanding, in the name of the church, "adequate international police forces."

But how is such a police force to be constituted and how is it to operate? How is it to be made strong enough to cope with attempts to disturb the international peace, should such occur, without becoming so strong as to constitute a threat to the liberties of the states within the society of nations? Most discussions of the postwar order are conspicuously silent or vague at this point. If their authors have considered it at all, they appear to have found it so difficult that they are content with some generalization about the need for an international police, after which they hasten on to some easier and more congenial subject.

It is the peculiar distinction of the postwar plan promoted by Mr. Ely Culbertson that he does at least present a full scheme for the organization of such a police force. It is a scheme without the slightest chance of adoption, for it is artfully designed to give military advantage to the United States and Great Britain — especially to the United States. Nevertheless, it deserves mention as one treatment of the postwar problem which does not dodge at a critical point.

It may be doubted, however, whether the problem of policing is as difficult as has been believed. There are, it seems to me, at least two considerations which must be kept in mind while considering it. One of these lies in the realm of political theory and the other in that of practical action. Both tend to simplify the problem.

Considered from the standpoint of political theory, it should be remembered that law and order obtain in our communities not because we have police, but because the overwhelming majority of citizens approve the laws and are ready to live as they require. "A police force," says Dr. Lorwin, "which attempts to uphold a state of affairs in which a significant portion of the community no longer acquiesces, is transformed from an impartial agent of politically organized society into the army of one class or group in a civil war. An international army can thus be compared to a police force in one respect. Neither of them can prevent war, international or civil, unless it is organized within a generally accepted and effectively functioning political and economic system. The horse and the cart are not interchangeable parts, even in this day of standardized production." [1]

Americans who remember what happened in the effort to enforce the Eighteenth Amendment will need no further argument with regard to the soundness of this contention. Its application to the operation of an international police is clear. If there is an international order in which the peoples find satisfaction for their present needs and hope for the future, a very small police force will suffice, since its services will be supported by the force of world public opinion. But if such an international order is lacking, no police force can maintain world order. Justice is the prior requirement.

From the standpoint of practical action, the problem equally depends on prior developments. If the close of fighting is swiftly followed by the disarmament of all belligerents, then it should be a comparatively simple matter to arrange for sufficient police forces to guard against the depredations of pirates and the rebuilding of military threats. (The issue will be still further simplified if the private armaments industry is abolished. Of that more later.) Former President Hoover is probably right in his contention that, in a disarmed world, a

---

[1] *Economic Consequences of the Second World War*, by Lewis L. Lorwin. New York: Random House, 1941. Quoted by permission.

very small air force under international direction could discharge all the policing functions required to keep the peace.

Given, therefore, the "generally accepted and effectively functioning political and economic system" covering all nations, and universal disarmament, and the difficulty in working out a system of international policing will virtually disappear. The requirement, as Dr. Lorwin intimates, is simply that the horse be kept ahead of the cart.

VII

This ideal of an inclusive world community, cooperatively formed and participated in by all nations and all peoples, which a prophetic church holds aloft as the way of peace, is not popular today. Even those who will acknowledge its attraction tend to dismiss it as beyond attainment until, perhaps, after millenniums more of agony and destruction and death, humanity has been bludgeoned into a new mind. A church that sees visions is dismissed as visionary. Especially in the United States, a nation which is discovering in this war the vastness of its power, the call is for realism. The mood of the moment is to demand that proposals for the future, leadership for the future, shall be 'realistic.' But what is realism?

Realism for the Secretary of the Navy is the possession of naval bases everywhere throughout the Pacific, and an American fleet strong enough to control the seven seas for a hundred years to come. Realism for Walter Lippmann is a Three Power Alliance of Russia, Great Britain and the United States, so strong that its word shall be law throughout the length and breadth of all the continents. If Russia refuses to enter such an alliance on terms which the other two nations will accept, then realism is an Anglo-American alliance, kept sufficiently strong in all its military branches to hold in check any aggregation of power Russia may assemble.

Realism for Clarence Streit and his " Union Now " disciples is another form of alliance between the Anglo-American peoples, with a united government wielding such authority that it can control the acts and fix the destiny of all the other nations. Realism for Henry R. Luce is recognition of the years that lie beyond the war as " The American Century," with the enormous resources of the United States used to control the economic — which in modern terms is to say, the political and social — fate of all the rest of the world. Realism for Colonel Robert R. McCormick is incorporation in the American federal union of the self-governing nations which now fly the British and Irish flags, so that the territory of the United States will belt the globe, and the giant power under the Stars and Stripes will no longer be the United States of America but the United States of the World.

These are proposals which men who bow at the shrine of realism are ready to discuss in these hours when the first radiant beams of a dazzling military victory begin to light the horizon. But the realism which they profess is sham. Every such scheme carries within itself the seeds of its own eventual doom. The powers which rely upon their military alliance to rule the earth are certain, and at no far distant time, to discover diversities of interests, conflicts of ambition, which will set in motion processes of internal intrigue. From that intrigue, seducing smaller nations to the support of one part of the alliance against its other parts, there will grow confusion, then suspicion, then the open break, then renewed warfare — and the last state of a world which has relied on this old, discredited means for keeping peace will be worse than the first. The power which relies on its own giant strength to bestride and hold in order the rest of mankind will only succeed, and in a few years, in driving its resentful subject nations into combinations, conspiracies, leagues pledged to liberation. Then will come uprising, the hopeless pouring out of the giant's strength to rule a globe — and catastrophe.   That is where such ' realism ' leads in the long run.

The Christian church must not compromise with any such deception.   It has its own realism — the realism of the moral law.   Moreover, it has that without which realism is a useless thing: it has vision — the vision of prophetic insight.   Vision and realism unite to make it proclaim that a just and lasting peace requires that a higher loyalty shall transcend our parochial national loyalties, that a true community of nations shall be established, that in the life and duties of that community all men, all races, all nations shall share.

CHAPTER IV

POWER POLITICS AND THE WORLD COMMUNITY

I

Few aphorisms have been worn more threadbare from frequent quotation than G. K. Chesterton's "Christianity has not been tried and found wanting; it has been found difficult and not tried." It occurs irresistibly to mind, however, because something much like that seems to have happened with respect to plans for a world federation in the coming peace. None of the hopes which were being so widely proclaimed in the early stages of the war has been proved unsound or removed from the realm of the possible. But as the difficulty of creating a true world community has grown more clear, men's desires have shriveled until today few seem to seek more from the war than a return to old-fashioned power politics, this time on a global scale.

What has caused this attrition? Undoubtedly many factors have played their parts, but one suspects that two in particular have exerted great influence.

In the first place, in the United States and Great Britain there has been a gradual awakening to the fact that the military outcome of the war, at least in Europe, would leave Russia in a position where Stalin could virtually dictate the terms of peace. The new map of Europe would be the map as Stalin ordered it drawn, and his Anglo-American allies would be in no position, without chancing an immediate break with the U.S.S.R., to make it otherwise. But Russia is known to fear

all federations which might, by any future political manipula-
tion, be forged into a *cordon sanitaire* such as conservative elements in England and America would gladly have seen thrown
about the communist state in the past. Therefore, there is
reason for those in the United States and Britain who are thinking about the nature of the postwar order to suspect that Russia will have slight sympathy for schemes of inclusive federation. Especially will this be true if such schemes are suspected
of concealing, however adroitly, the reservation of a preponderance of world power in the hands of the English-speaking
peoples.

More than this, the accumulation of difficulties once one goes
very far in thinking about methods of world organization has
damped much early enthusiasm. There are such differences in
levels of culture and living standards between continents, such
disparities in military strength and potential, such long historical roots for what seem now irrational rivalries and antipathies,
that the task of bringing all the nations into some sort of cooperative order, freely entered and gladly to be maintained,
grows to appear too baffling for human ingenuity and faith.
The attempt to form a world federation is found difficult and
not tried.

As a result, the peoples of the earth were brought up short
on March 21, 1943, by a radio address in which Winston
Churchill outlined the conception of a postwar order which
had taken form in his mind. The speech was instantly recognized as of highest importance, not simply because it gave the
first direct intimation from the head of the British government
of the postwar plans being contemplated by that government,
but because Mr. Churchill took this same occasion to make it
known that he hoped to continue in office after the war in order to carry into effect the plans thus revealed. (This despite
the fact that in his autobiography, *My Early Life,* Mr. Churchill
had said: " Those who can win a war well can rarely make a

good peace, and those who could make a good peace would never have won the war." [1])

Mr. Churchill's conception was very simple. "Under a world institution embodying or representing the United Nations, and some day all nations, there should come into being a Council of Europe and a Council of Asia." He said nothing further about the composition or powers of the latter, but the Council of Europe, he made it clear, should consist of "a council of great states and groups of [weaker] states" which "must eventually embrace the whole of Europe," and in which "the main branches of the European family must some day be partners." Apparently, this ambiguous phrase was designed to bring the United States into membership in this European council. "We must try," said Mr. Churchill, "to make the Council of Europe, or whatever it may be called, into a really effective league with all the strongest forces concerned woven into its texture, with a high court to adjust disputes and with forces, armed forces, national or international or both, held ready to enforce these decisions and prevent renewed aggression and the preparation of future wars."

Twenty days after Mr. Churchill's broadcast another forecast of the postwar shape of things reached the public from another high Allied source. In its April 10 issue the *Saturday Evening Post* published an article by one of its editors, Forrest Davis, outlining "Roosevelt's World Blueprint." The article claimed to have been authorized by the President; it quoted the President directly and with the utmost assurance attributed views of great definiteness to him; Mr. Davis had been used before to put the views of the administration on matters of foreign policy before the American people; this particular article has not, since its appearance, been disclaimed.

[1] Quoted in *Conditions of Peace*, by E. H. Carr, p. 244. The same point is made at great length and supported with a wealth of historical erudition by A. J. Toynbee in his *Study of History*, Vol. IV, pp. 298–300.

The Davis article must therefore be considered a dependable reflection of the views of the President of the United States on the nature of the postwar order, at least as he held them in April 1943.

According to " Roosevelt's World Blueprint," the President is determined that there shall be no revival of the League of Nations after the war, and no sort of international organization which might require any abatement of the sovereignty of the United States or the other victorious nations. He foresees the creation of a number of special commissions to carry on the tasks of rehabilitation which will confront the world at that time, and for the preservation of peace he would pledge the United Nations to a system of quarantine of aggressors, such as he first proposed in his famous Chicago speech of 1937.

President Roosevelt conceives this idea of national quarantines very literally. If a nation is held to be threatening the peace, and if it persists in that threat after having been warned (by a council of the victor nations?), then its borders should be closed, its rail, mail, telegraph and telephone communications cut off and its foreign trade stopped. If that does not bring it to its senses, it should be warned that aerial bombing will be the next step. And if *that* does not bring it to terms, it should be bombed. Apparently, the quarantining and bombing should be done by neighboring nations, using their own armed forces.

So far as any international organization is concerned, Mr. Roosevelt is credited with favoring something in the nature of the Pan-American Union. This is a loose federation of states, dominated by the overshadowing strength of the United States, which is doing much slowly to increase good will among the nations of the Americas (Canada has not become a member) and something, though by no means as much, to promote their economic integration. The extremely loose nature of the union is indicated by the fact that of 84 conventions and treaties so far adopted at sessions of the pan-American body, only 17 have been ratified by two-thirds of the 21 nations in the union.[2]

Analysis of the Churchill radio speech and the article outlining President Roosevelt's postwar intentions will show that neither gives more than lip service to the idea of a living world federation, neither is ready to contemplate any diminution of national sovereignty, and both are really thinking in terms of a new power politics. Mr. Churchill's postwar Europe is to be an alliance, a grouping of great powers, surrounded by satellite small states which must willy-nilly follow the lead which the big fellows lay down. Mr. Roosevelt's postwar world is to be a military agreement to use whatever force is required, first to isolate and then to blow to bits any nation which is adjudged a menace.[3] Now, carrying the argument to its logical conclusion, that influential publicist, Walter Lippmann, has presented his plea for a postwar order which shall be an explicit and undisguised military alliance of the dominant military powers as these emerge from the war.

II

Agreement seems to be general among political commentators that the appearance of Mr. Lippmann's book, *U. S. Foreign Policy: Shield of the Republic*, set up a new milestone along the path by which America is traveling into the postwar world. I am in entire agreement as to the book's importance, and that

[2] It should be apparent that President Roosevelt's plan for the quarantining of nations held to threaten world peace rests on certain very debatable assumptions. The way in which it would work if the would-be aggressor were Germany or Italy or Japan, especially after these have been disarmed, is plain. But why take it for granted that these represent the only future threats? How would such a scheme work if aggression were threatened by Russia or China?

[3] Again we ask, Adjudged by whom? And on the basis of what tests? The *Saturday Evening Post* article embodying President Roosevelt's views is unfortunately vague at this vital point.

not simply because of the almost unprecedented distribution which it has gained. It has been circulated to half a million readers by the Book-of-the-Month Club and by bookstore sales. It has been presented, in somewhat compressed form, to the seven (or is it eleven?) million readers of *Reader's Digest*. The *Ladies Home Journal* has devoted seven pages to a picturization of its contents, thoughtfully arranged in cartoon form for women who are much too busy with war work to read Mr. Lippmann's actual words. Presently it will be serialized in hundreds of daily papers, and it is rumored that Hollywood is planning to make a Disneyesque feature of its ideas.

No postwar program which has been circulated on this scale is to be lightly regarded. Yet in this case, one feels that the appearance of this book is of even greater importance than its sales suggest because of what it indicates as to the change of thinking now going on in the minds of American leaders with regard to the postwar prospect. Advertisements of the book carry the enthusiastic commendation of Americans as different in viewpoint as Wendell Willkie, William Allen White and John Chamberlain. Mr. Lippmann has himself been identified in the past with the school of thought on American foreign policy which largely found its inspiration in the 'internationalism' of Woodrow Wilson. He recognizes and seeks to excuse himself for this in the opening pages of his preface. If this book truly represents the postwar program of American liberalism, then that program, it must be recognized, will be an essay in unabashed power politics.

For Mr. Lippmann has a crystal-clear thesis, which he presents with a directness, a scorn of subterfuge, that adds much to his book's persuasiveness. A solvent foreign policy, he holds, "consists in bringing into balance, with a comfortable surplus of power in reserve, the nation's commitments and the nation's power." When he says "foreign commitment" he means "an obligation outside the continental limits of the

United States which may in the last analysis have to be met by waging war." When he uses the term "power" he means "the force which is necessary to prevent such a war or to win it if it cannot be prevented." [4]   To discharge our commitments after this war, and to keep the peace, the United States should join a permanent, formal, military alliance with Great Britain and Russia.

This proposal for a three-power military alliance to rule the world, Mr. Lippmann seeks to make palatable to American liberals by two devices. First, he is careful to speak of it as a "nuclear" alliance, which plants the idea that it is to be only a core around which a genuine and inclusive world community may form. Second, he says that China, "if possible," should be included in the nuclear alliance.

But these provisions in reality mean nothing. The alliance is to be nuclear in name only; if it came into existence other nations would perforce have to range themselves around it, but there is no provision in Mr. Lippmann's blueprint for any transfer of power from the Big Three. Indeed, his program rests on the assumption that the Big Three shall keep and exercise world power. And the gesture in China's direction is purely verbal, since this is an alliance of *powers* and Mr. Lippmann makes it clear that China is not yet (although potentially) a power. The test, for Mr. Lippmann, is military might. China cannot be made a full partner in this scheme for ruling the postwar world because she "is not yet an arsenal." France, incidentally, is ruled out on the same basis — because she does not "possess the resources to become a principal arsenal." That, in brief, is what is involved in the Lippmann proposal — world peace enforced by an alliance of the "arsenal" nations.

It hardly needs to be pointed out that this is naked power

---

[4] From *U. S. Foreign Policy: Shield of the Republic*, by Walter Lippmann. Boston: Little, Brown & Company, 1943. All quotations by permission of the publishers.

politics. It is power politics on a scale undreamed even by Metternich and Talleyrand. It may look like 'realism' at first glance, but it contains two fatal flaws. In the first place, it assumes a continuing identity of interest between Russia and the two other members of the alliance which is unlikely to exist — or at least to exist long. In the second place, it fails to propose any solution for the colonial problem in Asia, but would expect the billion people of that continent to acquiesce in a return to the colonial *status quo ante*, except in the case of the Japanese colonies, the one non-European colonial system hitherto in existence.

To realize Mr. Lippmann's failure to grasp and solve the Russian problem, the reader should study with care the entire eighth chapter in his book. Particular attention should be given the material on pages 146–52. Mr. Lippmann contends that the test of Russia's intentions will come immediately at the close of the war in her treatment of the region running from Finland on the north through Poland, the Danubian nations, the Balkan nations, to Turkey. " If," he writes, " in this region the effort to settle territorial boundaries and to decide what governments shall be recognized discloses deep and insoluble conflicts between Russia's conception of her vital interests and that of the Western Allies, then every nation will know that it must get ready and must choose sides in the eventual but unavoidable next war." And Mr. Lippmann is astute enough to know that in this region Great Britain and the United States will be helpless. " The region lies beyond the reach of American power." " Does this mean that Poland, the Danubian states and the Balkan states have no prospect of assured independence and that they are destined inexorably to become satellites of Russia or to be incorporated into the Soviet Union? *The question cannot be answered categorically at this time*." (I cannot resist italicizing that sentence.) " It would seem that the hope of a good settlement on Russia's western borderlands depends upon whether the border states will adopt a policy of neutralization, and whether Russia will accept and support it." So it will be seen that Mr. Lippmann's three-power alliance rests on two very sizable *ifs*, with a third World War — Britain-America vs. the U.S.S.R. — if either of these fails to work out in the manner he hopes.

Even this, however, does not fully disclose the nature of the Russian problem for the alliance Mr. Lippmann has in view. After all, is it true that the treatment of Finland, Poland and the Danubian and Balkan states is *the* key to Europe's future? (It is one key, make no mistake about that.) Is not the post-war treatment of Germany likely to have an even greater influence on the duration of the coming peace? Yet is there not a fundamental difference in the approach which Britain and Russia can make to this particular problem which almost insures that Germany will be thrown into the Russian orbit? Is not Britain, in the nature of the case, bound to be interested in the suppression of Germany as a manufacturing and shipping rival, while Russia can well afford to encourage the development of Germany so long as there is any possibility of gearing her into the Russian economy as the manufacturing arsenal of Soviet-Socialist power? With this fundamental divergence of interest in the heart of Europe, and with Mr. Lippmann's admission of Russia's impregnability in her geopolitical " Heartland," what are the long-term prospects of the three-power alliance?

Mr. Lippmann's treatment of the postwar problem in the Pacific is so brief that one suspects he has given it little thought. Certainly what hints he holds forth suggest little understanding of the elemental forces which have been undermining the colonial order. It is not simply the extension of Japan's empire which is at stake in the Far East. As Chiang Kai-shek, Asia's spokesman, has made clear, the peoples of Asia want an end to all empires. They are quite as determined to do away with the European colonial order as with Japan's effort to establish a Greater Asia Co-Prosperity Sphere. And in this determination they will certainly have the support of Russia, in herself the largest Asiatic power, if there remains alive in Russia a vestige of her original revolutionary impulse. Yet Mr. Lippmann apparently expects that his victorious three powers will turn right around, after Japan has been defeated and stripped of her loot, and restore the European colonial system as it existed before the war! And that Russia, China and all the peoples in European colonies will accept this revived colonial order as though Hongkong and Singapore had never been!

III

At this point it seems high time to say something about the alleged ' realism ' of power politics. The trouble with Mr. Lippmann's proposal, and with almost all schemes which rest upon the concentration of overwhelming military power in some alliance or council or other combination of victor nations, is that they assume a continuation of identity of interest between these nations. The factors which have forced them together to win a victory are assumed to be strong enough to hold them together over a long stretch of peace. There could be no more baseless assumption. That is why there is a certain mocking logic about the proposal made by Colonel Robert R. McCormick, of the *Chicago Tribune*, for postwar incorporation of most of the rest of the world in the American federal union. Colonel McCormick of course made his proposal with his tongue in his cheek. But it is difficult to pick the logical flaw in the argument that, to insure the identity of interest requisite to make a system of world control by power politics work, the simplest and most effective step would be to include everybody in one nation — and that, naturally, the United States!

History has some sobering words to offer at this point, if we will only listen. How long did Britain and France find their interests identical after 1918? They had begun to fall apart before the adjournment of the Paris Peace Conference. In his too little known memoirs of the conference and the period immediately after, *Grandeur and Misery of Victory*, Georges Clemenceau relates an incident worth recalling:

On my return from India, as I was passing through London on my way to Oxford to receive an honorary degree, Mr. Lloyd George asked me to come to see him at the House of Commons. His first words were to ask me if I had anything to say to him.

' Yes, indeed! ' I replied. ' I have to tell you that from the very day after the Armistice I found you an enemy to France.'

' Well,' he rejoined, ' *was it not always our traditional policy?* ' [5]

This might be dismissed as a cynical jest employed by the protean Welshman to turn the point of an attack which he did not care to meet squarely, and given too sinister an import by the French premier. But the whole balance of power policy, which has fixed the nature of European politics since the days of Louis XIV, has rested on the ability of Britain to shift its support from one continental state to another as its own immediate interests have seemed to shift.

A few years before the present war I heard Winston Churchill speak in a Chicago club. In the question period which followed the address someone asked, " Mr. Churchill, I am unable to understand Britain's foreign policy. Can you explain it for me? " Instantly came the reply: " That's very simple. Britain always supports the second power on the Continent."

It is difficult to see, in the light of Germany's impending disarmament and France's catastrophe, how this traditional bal-

[5] From *Grandeur and Misery of Victory*, by Georges Clemenceau. New York: Harcourt, Brace & Company, 1930. Quoted by permission. The italics are Clemenceau's.

ance of power policy is to be continued by Great Britain after the war.[6] But as a commentary on any postwar policy based on an assumption of continued identity of interests between war allies, both Mr. Churchill's and Mr. Lloyd George's remarks have their point.

Moreover, any candid survey of the situation as it exists *now*, while the war is still in progress, should cast doubt on the soundness of such an assumption. This is hardly a matter on which one wishes to dilate at length at the present juncture, but for the sake of straight thinking we must at least glance at a few facts. How truly united, even today, are the United Nations?

Consider, for example, American fears of postwar Britain. Who can deny that a considerable portion of the American public, and by no means the least intelligent portion, has a well formed fear that it has become a prime object of British policy after the war to involve the United States in underwriting the defense of the far-flung empire which, as this war is demonstrating, Britain herself can no longer defend alone? On July 13 of the present year Colonel Oliver Stanley told Parliament that the Churchill government is now formulating plans whereby, while the control of her colonies will remain securely in the hands of Britain, other nations having an interest in their welfare would, after the war, be invited to assist in their economic development. Still later, a group of fourteen British church leaders, including the two Anglican archbishops, in approving the Six Pillars formulated by an American church body, added to its approval of the fourth — autonomy for subject peoples and an international organization to assure and supervise its realization — the proviso that administration of

---

[6] It is, of course, possible for Britain to conceive a postwar balance of power policy in terms of her relations with Russia and the United States, shifting her weight to the weaker side as the international situation moves from one crisis to another. It is simply in terms of *Continental* politics after the war that a British balance of power policy seems out of the question.

each piece of subject territory by single nations is still the best system. But, these British church leaders added, " under modern conditions it has become improbable that even the strongest single power will continue to be able to defend and develop dependencies single-handed." Which led the *Christian Century* to comment: " So by coincidence these churchmen come out at the very place where Colonel Stanley comes out. His formula: Britain rules, America finances, both defend."

Perhaps even more Americans have a fear lest British postwar policy seek to obtain American underwriting for whatever course the London government may elect to follow with regard to Moscow. It is mainly over the possibility of a clash between what are held to be British interests on the Continent or in Asia and Russian interests that these Americans fear that the United States might become involved in war with the U.S.S.R.

Equally real are British fears of the United States. These take at least two major forms. There is, first of all, the pervasive fear, for which only too much ground exists, that at the end of the war the United States may again seek to draw back into its own hemispheric shell, leaving England to carry the burden of postwar reorganization in Europe without American support. In which case, to an even greater degree than is admitted by Mr. Lippmann, Britain would find herself virtually helpless in the hands of Stalin. And in the second place, there is the growing fear felt by many powerful British business interests that the United States will use certain advantages it has gained during the war to grab a dominant position in world trade, finance and communications. The more than acidulous speeches made in both the British Parliament and the American Congress on the prospects for postwar aviation should serve to make this fear, as it exists on both sides of the Atlantic, clear.

Or consider British fears of Russia. Does anyone imagine that Tory England has no misgivings about its postwar relations with the Soviet Union? What if western Europe should go communist? It easily may. Even if Russia makes no overt moves to bring this to pass, the very political vacuum which may exist after the war in countries like Germany, France and Spain, plus the presence in those countries of organized and disciplined Communist parties with determined leadership and fully worked out programs, plus the mere presence in Europe of the tremendously powerful Soviet Union, may produce communist crises all over the Continent. What of Russia in Asia? Is India any more safe from communist penetration than it was from tsarist advances in the days when Kipling was warning his countrymen against " Adam-zad, the bear that walks like a man "? Is Burma? Is Malaya? Is Afghanistan, and the Moslem territory along the Red Sea and the Suez Canal?

What must be the thoughts now of any British believer in the sanctity of the empire who has become even partially convinced of the truth of the formula laid down by Sir Halford Mackinder and the school of geopoliticians who follow in his train? We are all familiar with that formula: " Who rules eastern Europe commands the Heartland. Who rules the Heartland commands the World Island. Who rules the World Island commands the world." [7] But what is the portent of such a formula for the period after the war when the U.S.S.R. will rule almost exactly this territory which has been discovered to be the Heartland?

One of the most curious articles to appear recently was published in the quarterly, *Foreign Affairs*, for July 1943, by Professor Mackinder. The editors had asked the octogenarian geographer whether the developments of the war had in any way undermined his theory of Heartland, World Island and world. He wrote to argue that, on the contrary, they had

[7] Cf. *Democratic Ideals and Reality*, by Halford J. Mackinder. New York: Henry Holt & Company, 1919 and 1942.

added new proof of the correctness of his formula. But I call the article curious because there is in it no apparent recognition of the fact that one outcome of the war will almost certainly be to place Russia in undisputed control of this key territory to world control — if geopolitics is correct — which Hitler has sacrificed millions of German lives and the peace of the world to seize. Perhaps Sir Halford sees that fact plainly enough. One suspects that a geopolitician of his perspicacity must do so. But evidently he does not care to discuss its implications.

Or consider Russian fears of Britain and the United States. Here one must bear in mind not only the misbegotten intervention of 1919–20, the frequent disclosure in influential British and American quarters of ill will for the communist experiment, but even more the heritage of years of indoctrination, as a fundamental postulate of Communist party doctrine, that a day will come when the Soviet Union will be forced to repel a final gigantic attempt by the capitalist world to destroy the Marx-Leninist state. Max Eastman, in an article in *Reader's Digest* for July 1943, quoted ominous words from the 1939 revision of Stalin's book, *Problems of Leninism*, which, as he says, is quite as much the inspired scripture of Communism as *Mein Kampf* has been of Nazism:

What is the meaning of the impossibility of complete and final victory of socialism in a single country without the victory of the revolution in other countries? It means the impossibility of having full guarantees against intervention, and hence against the restoration of the bourgeois order. . . . To deny this indisputable fact is to abandon Leninism. " We are living," Lenin writes, " not merely in a state, but in a *system of states;* and it is inconceivable that the Soviet republic shall continue to exist for a long period side by side with imperialist states. *Ultimately one or the other must conquer.*" [8]

---

[8] The italics are Stalin's.

With the experience of Munich only five years in the past, with books and articles appearing which betray Anglo-American dreams of world control, with the multiplying indications of American ambitions in the Pacific, how can Russia help but be apprehensive about the postwar policies of her capitalist allies?

Or finally, consider China's fears of everybody. No more meaningful declaration has come out of the war than that addressed to the forum of the *New York Herald Tribune* on November 17, 1942, by the Chinese generalissimo, Chiang Kaishek. Its importance justifies an extended quotation:

There will be neither peace, nor hope, nor future for any of us unless we honestly aim at political, social and economic justice for all peoples of the world, great and small. But I feel confident that we of the United Nations can achieve that aim only by starting at once to organize an international order embracing all peoples to enforce peace and justice among them. To make that start we must begin today and not tomorrow to apply these principles among ourselves, even at some sacrifice to the absolute powers of our individual countries. We should bear in mind one of the most inspiring utterances of the last World War, that of Edith Cavell: "Standing at the brink of the grave, I feel that patriotism alone is not enough."

We Chinese are not so blind as to believe that the new international order will usher in the millennium. But we do not look upon it as visionary. The idea of universal brotherhood is innate in the catholic nature of Chinese thought; it was the dominant concept of Dr. Sun Yat-sen, whom events have proved time and again to be not a visionary but one of the world's greatest realists.

Among our friends there has recently been some talk of China emerging as the leader of Asia, as if China wished the mantle of an unworthy Japan to fall on her shoulders. Having herself been a victim of exploitation, China has infinite sympathy for the submerged nations of Asia, and toward them China feels she has only responsibilities — not rights. We repudiate the idea of leadership of Asia because the "führer principle" has been synonymous with domination and exploitation, precisely as the " East Asia co-prosperity sphere " has stood for a race of mythical supermen lording over groveling subject races.

China has no desire to replace Western imperialism in Asia with an Oriental imperialism or isolationism of its own or of anyone else. We hold that we must advance from the narrow idea of exclusive alliances and regional blocs which in the end make for bigger and better wars, to effective organization of world unity. Unless real world cooperation replaces both isolationism and imperialism of whatever form in the new interdependent world of free nations, there is no lasting security for you or for us.

IV

Chiang Kai-shek is a more realistic world statesman than Mr. Lippmann, or than any of the advocates of a postwar order based on a power politics alliance against whom he was obviously leveling his shafts. The truth is that to organize a world community on the basis of military alliance is no easier task than to organize such a community on the free and inclusive basis advocated by the Chinese leader. It would probably prove not so easy. And the long-term prospects of such a power politics alliance are for progressive disintegration and descent into another hell of war. While the long-term prospects of the sort of world community envisaged by Chiang Kai-shek are for progressive integration and ascent to a new level of international life in which peace will become the common concern of all.

Since the success of the power quest is so doubtful, why should not the demand for the cooperative quest be insistently sounded? Why accept the timidities and shortsightedness of tired political leaders as final? Why not meet youth with the challenge of the great end, the end which in our deepest hearts we all know we should be seeking. (Youth is already cynical of the leadership of national governments and skeptical of power pact proposals. Are we to surrender it to such cynicism? If we do, we surrender the future.)

Most of all, since I am addressing primarily the Christian church, let this question be faced: Is it not the business of the church in this realm to keep alive the demand, not for what it is told can be, but for what its own vision of a better world tells it should be?

CHAPTER V

WHAT OF THE EMPIRES?

I

From Chungking, China, on an October day in 1942, there flashed to the world an interview with a traveling American which caused government officials in Washington and London — and in other capitals as well — to sit up with a start. Wendell L. Willkie, titular leader of the Republican party in the United States, had reached the Chinese capital on a tour of the war fronts in which he was eventually to cover 31,000 miles in forty-nine days. As he made his way from Accra to Cairo, and on to Teheran, Kuibishev, Tashkent and Chengtu, the dimensions and immediacy of the colonial problem began to press in on him. Somewhere between Moscow and Chungking he saw a great light.

In all the countries which he had visited, Mr. Willkie told his interviewers, the common people hoped that the United Nations would win the war. But all hoped that after the war they could live in freedom. And "they all doubt, in varying degree, the readiness of the leading democracies of the world to stand up and be counted for freedom for others after the war is over."

Then this American, who was meeting the colonial question at first hand for the first time and seeing it as it appears in the eyes of thoughtful Asiatics, went on to say such things as this:

The truth is that we as a nation have not made up our minds what kind of world we want to speak for when victory comes. Especially here in Asia the common people feel that we have

asked them to join us for no better reason than that Japanese rule
would be even worse than Western imperialism. . . . Freedom
and opportunity are the words which have modern magic for the
people of Asia, and we have let the Japanese — the most cruel im-
perialists the modern world has known — steal these words from
us and corrupt them to their own uses. . . .

Mr. Willkie then called for a Pacific Charter which would
make unmistakably clear the postwar intentions in the Far East
of the nations which formulated the Atlantic Charter. Then
he continued:

Some of the plans to which such a statement would lead are already clear, I deeply believe, to most Americans.

We believe this war must mean an end to the empire of nations
over other nations. No foot of Chinese soil, for example, should
be or can be ruled from now on except by the people who live
on it. And we must say so *now*, not after the war.

We believe it is the world's job to find some system for helping
colonial peoples who join the United Nations' cause to become free
and independent nations. We must set up firm timetables under
which they can work out and train governments of their own
choosing, and we must establish ironclad guarantees, administered
by all the United Nations jointly, that they shall not slip back into
colonial status.

Only the Colonel Blimp mentality, one would think, could
touch the Orient today and not be aware of this omnipresent
demand for freedom. Surely it should not have taken recent
events in Malaya, in Burma and in Indonesia — with the con-
trasting events in the Philippines — to show that as between a
future under an Asiatic and one under a European imperialism,
the peoples of the East are indifferent. Despite all the material
advantages which we may claim have been conferred by colonial rule, they put the blessing of liberty before all other bless-
ings.

This demand for independence, for liberation from European control, rises all the way across this largest of continents, from Syria to the China Sea, and spills over into the islands of the Pacific. It has been growing ever since little Japan defied and defeated the Russian giant in 1905. (Americans and Britons went into tumults of rejoicing at that victory, never dreaming what it presaged.) If you would grasp the universality and power of this demand for Asiatic freedom today, turn back and read again the words of Chiang Kai-shek which closed the preceding chapter.

If we could project ourselves a hundred years into the future, and read the historians of 2043, I believe that we would find them treating the Japanese campaign which reached its climax in the capture of Singapore as one of the most important military campaigns in recorded history. Important, that is, in its psychological and long-range effects. Japan's occupation of Singapore will be short-lived. But the blow which Japan administered to white prestige when it captured with such consummate ease the base which had been hailed as " the Gibraltar of the East," was a blow from which white pretensions to impregnability and unchallengeable power will never recover.

For a little time after Singapore it looked as though the lessons of that defeat might be grasped by Western nations. Thus the London *Times*, in a remarkable editorial which admitted that the capitulation was " the greatest blow which has befallen the British Empire since the loss of the American colonies," went on to express the hope that, like the loss of America, the fall of Singapore might bring drastic changes in British overseas policy:

That the past is dead beyond recall has been clearly recognized for a quarter-century by British opinion and by British statesmen in their dealings both with China and with India. New principles have been proclaimed, and have found expression in policy. But the progress toward their full realization — sometimes in China, more often in India — was grudging and faltering.

Lack of imagination, insufficient flexibility, too much attention to past traditions and established interests, prevented that revolutionary and wholehearted reorientation of British policy and outlook which could alone have equipped us to meet the hurricane in the Far East and is now the first condition for recovery.

While it will come as a surprise to most Chinese and Indians to learn that British statesmanship and public opinion have been agreed for a quarter-century that past imperialistic policies were " dead beyond recall," there is nevertheless meaning in the call of such a conservative organ as the *Times* for a " revolutionary and wholehearted reorientation of British policy " in the colonial world. But just how much meaning? As the days have gone by since Singapore, and as the doom of Japan's ambitions has grown more certain, such expressions as this in the *Times*, or that by Mr. Willkie, have grown infrequent.

Japan has seized a vast empire in the East — an empire exceeded in size only by that of Great Britain, and in wealth possibly surpassing even that. Yet Japan will be unable to hold this empire. The forces arrayed against her are too strong; her lines of communication are too extended and too exposed; her resources are still too limited. She will be defeated. She may be subjected to the most complete destruction of her cities and manufacturing centers in the annals of modern war. Her armies will be forced to withdraw from China, Korea, Formosa. Her navy will be sunk; her air force shattered. Then what is to happen in the Orient? When the Japanese forces have completed that long retreat, who is to occupy where they have evacuated? A year, five years, after Japan has capitulated, will Asia and the Pacific islands present the picture of the old imperialistic order, restored just as it was before this storm?

It is possible that that will come to pass. Unless Russia im-

poses her veto — an unlikely prospect during the years immediately after the war when the Soviet Union will be rebuilding
its ravaged territories and renewing its war potential — it
should be no great task for a victorious United States and
England to re-establish substantially the same colonial order
that Japan has overthrown. How long that order could be
maintained and at what cost — all that is another matter. But
for the time being it could be restored. If, however, that
comes to pass, then the United States will stand discredited
forever in the eyes of the East. For America will appear to
the peoples of Asia to have entered the war in the name of
freedom, and come out of it having fastened new chains on
those whose highest aspiration it is to be free.

II

Hitler's war for *Lebensraum* has become the greatest colonial war in history. Turn to any of the maps which constantly
appear in the press locating the principal bases occupied by
American troops and this should at once become evident. Of
the thirty or forty localities thus identified by small American
flags, or some other nationalistic symbols, the overwhelming
majority will be found in colonial territory. In Central and
North Africa, in the Near East, in the Middle East, in Eritrea,
in India, in Burma, in the Philippines, in the islands of the
southwest Pacific, in Hawaii, in the Aleutians, in Alaska, yes,
even in China — the places where American forces are fighting
or are preparing to fight are the outposts of empire. That is
more than a coincidence.

Six of the great empires — British, French, Dutch, Portu-
guese, Italian and American — have lost territory since the war
started.[1] One empire, the Japanese, has immensely swollen
in size. The Netherlands Indies, French Indo-China, Malaya,

[1] Portugal, although a neutral, has lost colonial holdings at Macao and
Timor islands.

Burma, much of China, many Pacific islands including the Philippines, Libya, Tunisia, Ethiopia, Eritrea, Italian Somaliland, Madagascar, Crete and (temporarily) Kiska and Attu have changed hands. New defense arrangements, whose ultimate political consequences can now be only conjectured, have been put into effect in the British, Dutch and French colonies in the Caribbean and western Atlantic. Syria, Iran, Irak have found themselves involved in military occupations which left their political future in grave doubt. India has seen thousands of nationalists imprisoned; world figures such as Mohandas Gandhi and Jawaharlal Nehru are still held incommunicado.

What this means is that the entire colonial structure, evolved by the imperialism of the three preceding centuries, has been torn to pieces and is now, in the language of the street, " up for grabs." More than a billion and a half people look to the end of the war to learn their political fate. What disposition will be made of these vast territories?

At this point one thinks first of the Atlantic Charter. That document, jointly issued by President Roosevelt and Prime Minister Churchill, opens with the assurances:

First, their countries seek no aggrandizement, territorial or other.

Second, they desire to see no territorial changes that do not accord with the freely expressed wishes of the peoples concerned.

Third, they respect the right of all peoples to choose the form of government under which they live; and they wish to see sovereign rights and self-government restored to those who have been forcibly deprived of them.

But from the beginning there has been question as to the extent to which the Atlantic Charter applied to the colonial world, especially in the Orient. Mr. Churchill threw doubt upon its applicability when, in interpreting the charter to the British Parliament within a month after its publication, he seemed specifically to exempt India and Burma from its operations, and added: "At the Atlantic meeting we had in mind primarily the extension of the sovereignty, self-government and national life of the states and nations of Europe now under the Nazi yoke and the principles which should govern any alterations in the territorial boundaries of countries which may have to be made. That is quite a separate problem from the progressive evolution of self-governing institutions in regions whose people owe allegiance to the British crown."

Since that time, self-appointed interpreters have occasionally sought to make it appear that the British Prime Minister's words did not actually rule out the application of the principles of the charter to India and former British colonies now occupied by the enemy. But Mr. Churchill has made no effort to clear up the ambiguity — if ambiguity it is — created by his words, though more than two years have passed, though constant demands have been made that he should do so, and though he has never found it difficult to make his meaning clear when he so desired. On the contrary, he has if anything added to the impression of intransigence on the colonial issue by the subsequent speech in which he brusquely announced that he had not become the king's first minister to preside at the liquidation of the British Empire and flatly declared, "What is ours we hold."

Nor is Mr. Churchill to be regarded as alone in his attitude on the imperialistic issue. At Edinburgh on May 8, 1942, the British foreign minister, Anthony Eden, made a speech to which too little attention has been paid, especially since Viscount Simon, the British lord chancellor, went out of his way to inform the House of Lords that it expressed the future colonial policy of the British government. Said Mr. Eden:

You cannot run a large colonial empire well unless you are determined to do so, and unless you are proud to make the necessary sacrifices to carry through the task. In that period between the two wars, in which our intentions were so excellent and our purpose was so woefully weak, we almost became shy of the fact that we were entrusted with a vast empire. That must never happen again. I use the word entrusted advisedly. Our purpose in developing our colonial empire must not be to gain commercial advantage for ourselves nor to exploit transient commercial opportunities. Still less should we seek to uproot native habits of life. It must be our privilege to develop our colonial empire, to raise the standard of life of the many races dwelling in it, to gain their confidence, their trust, their free collaboration in the work we have both to do. This means that men and women must be ready to give up their working lives to this service. This same colonial empire has given us the lives and work of many of its sons and daughters during the war. We pledge ourselves not to fail them in the period after the war.

Did this whittling away of the promises of the Atlantic Charter come as an unpleasant surprise to the United States government? There are signs that it did.

On February 23, 1942, President Roosevelt specifically assured the peoples of Asia that " the Atlantic Charter applies not only to parts of the world that border the Atlantic but to the whole world: disarmament of aggressors, self-determination of nations and peoples, and the Four Freedoms." And on Memorial Day, only about three weeks after Mr. Eden's Edinburgh speech, the American undersecretary of state (at that time acting secretary), Sumner Welles, said at the tomb of the Unknown Soldier:

Our victory must bring in its train the liberation of all peoples. Discrimination between peoples because of their race, creed or color must be abolished. The age of imperialism is ended. The right of a people to their freedom must be recognized.

And along with this there should be remembered the statement made by Stalin on November 6, 1942, the twenty-fifth anniversary of the Bolshevist revolution. As Mr. Willkie has

pointed out, " it is a singularly explicit and exact statement."
Stalin declared that Russia was fighting for —

Abolition of racial exclusiveness, equality of nations and integrity of their territories, liberation of enslaved nations and restoration of their sovereign rights, the right of every nation to arrange its affairs as it wishes, economic aid to nations that have suffered and assistance to them in attaining their material welfare, restoration of democratic liberties, the destruction of the Hitlerite regime.

III

In this murky realm of colonial policy, with the fate of so many millions at stake, with the declarations of the warring powers capable of such contradictory interpretations, has the Christian church anything to say?

It assuredly has. Just before the outbreak of the war, at a time when it had become clear that imperialistic pressures were doing much to drive the world toward catastrophe, the World Council of Churches, even though it had not then completed its formation, brought together in Geneva, Switzerland, a commission of " lay experts " to formulate general principles on which to deal with the colonial problem. The members of that group were drawn from many parts of Europe and Asia, as well as from Britain and America. Under such church auspices they formulated these recommendations:

1. That indigenous peoples must not be treated as pawns of international policy;

2. That the paramount aim of the governments concerned must be the moral, social and material welfare of the native population, as well as native autonomy as comprehensive as the conditions of each territory allow, to the end that ultimately the population of the area may be able to assume responsibility for its own destiny;

3. That native institutions and, in particular, the systems of land tenure be used and developed;

4. That missionary work be freely allowed;

5. That the denial of essential rights upon the basis of race dis-

crimination be recognized as inconsistent with the welfare of the governed peoples;

6. That the militarization of native peoples be forbidden;

7. That political propaganda in colonial territories for foreign purposes be recognized as injurious to native society;

8. That the principle of economic equality be recognized, subject always to the paramount claims of native economic welfare;

9. That such a system be carried out under the effective supervision of an international body, whose members shall be independent of national control.

The applicability of these recommendations, especially to some of the conditions and policies which have grown up in colonies in Africa, hardly needs to be pointed out. But since the outbreak of the war, and the emergence of the colonial problem in the exaggerated form already discussed, church bodies have begun to speak in even more determined and prophetic tones. Consider, for example, this seventh of the " Guiding Principles " laid down by the Delaware Conference:

We believe that that government which derives its just powers from the consent of the governed is the truest expression of the rights and dignity of man. This requires that we seek autonomy for all subject and colonial peoples. Until that shall be realized, the task of colonial government is no longer one of exclusive national concern. It must be recognized as a common responsibility of mankind, to be carried out in the interests of the colonial peoples by the most appropriate form of organization. This would, in many cases, make colonial government a task of international collaboration for the benefit of colonial peoples who would, themselves, have a voice in their government. As the agencies for the promotion of world-wide political and economic security become effective, the moral, social and material welfare of colonial populations can be more fully realized.

And further, in dealing with the future of peoples not yet ready to assume the responsibilities of full self-government, the Delaware Conference declared:

That, utilizing experience with the mandate principle, a system of administration of colonial territories under international authority be developed. In areas now under colonial administration, advance toward self-government should be carried forward in substantial progress. The affairs of peoples deemed not yet capable of self-government should be administered as a common trust, by international authority, in the interest of these peoples as members of a world society.

Finally, to complete the record, consider the fourth of the "Six Pillars of Peace," as formulated by the Commission to Study the Bases of a Just and Durable Peace of the Federal Council of Churches:

The peace must proclaim the goal of autonomy for subject peoples, and it must establish international organization to assure and to supervise the realization of that end.

It is unfortunate that the Princeton Conference, containing as it did at least a few delegates from regions where the imperialistic issue is most exigent, should have remained silent on the future of colonies. Perhaps the very large proportion of delegates from portions of the British Empire was not unrelated to that silence. The caveat filed by prominent English clergy against the fourth Peace Pillar, just quoted, has already been mentioned.[2]

What, then, is the conception of the future of empires held forth by the church? In its prophetic utterance the church calls, first, for the abrogation of the principle of imperialism. There must be henceforth no possession of colonies with a view to lasting ownership and privileged exploitation. There must be no empires which are conceived as beyond liquidation. Instead, all colonies must be held in trust for their peoples, and all must be conceived as in progress of evolution toward freedom. Where possible, freedom must be granted at once.

[2] See pages 72–73.

Where that is not possible, freedom must be the acknowledged goal; colonial status must be regarded as no more than a temporary and passing phase.

In the second place, there must be genuine education for self-government. There must be what Mr. Willkie has called "firm timetables" by which to carry out and speed progress away from dependency. The steps by which nationals are to be given increasing responsibility for colonial administration are to be made clear in advance, and the aspirations of patriotic youth are to be met, not by vague words and empty promises, but by definite proposals for the progressive transfer of authority with complete autonomy in view at some specified point.

In the third place, the system of national colonial holdings must give way to an international system which, conceivably, might take two forms. On the one hand, the churches propose that colonies be held and administered by international bodies — " a task of international collaboration for the benefit of colonial peoples." It is this suggestion which seems to have aroused the most indignation in Tory circles in Great Britain. Yet it has much to commend it if the intention of the Western nations is truly to do away with the faults of the imperialistic order. On the other hand, it is held that certain national holdings of colonies might persist provided that these were under international supervision. In which case, to recall Mr. Eden's emphasized verb, colonies would indeed be " entrusted " to the nations administering them, but the trust would be granted by some international authority which would require that the trustee render frequent account of the manner in which his obligation was being discharged.

Which brings us to the question of mandates. Mandates are in poor repute at present because of the history of the mandatories between the close of the Paris Peace Conference and the outbreak of the present war. The sorry truth is, of course, that certain nations consented to adopt the mandatory principle at Paris only to satisfy President Wilson's insistence that wartime pledges against annexations be kept. They believed at the time that it would be possible, after obtaining coveted territories as mandates, to treat them as colonies, and the event proved their expectations sound. The authority of the League of Nations was continually flouted by the mandatory powers. As the mandate system worked from 1920 to 1939, it was essentially the old imperialism under a new name.

Nevertheless, the church believes that there is still value in the mandate principle. The Delaware Conference called for its revival; its specific proposal (see page 89) lends itself easily to the interpretation that *all* colonies, whether or not spoils of war, should be placed under some sort of mandate administration. And as a means of guarding against any such perversion of the mandate system as followed the last war, would it not be well to consider the possibility of joint mandates or of the administration of mandated territories by administrators drawn from many countries? If, for example, it should be decided to deal with the vexing problem of Indo-China by placing that region, for a period of political tutelage, under a mandate, why not escape imperialistic pitfalls by giving the mandate jointly to such neighbors as China and the Philippines? Or if Palestine is to continue to be administered by mandate for a time after the war, why not free that whole administration from the suspicion of being primarily concerned with British imperial interests by turning the administration over to a group of trained experts from, say, Switzerland, Norway and Brazil?

IV

When the Christian church begins to talk in this way concerning the future of what has been the colonial system, is all that it says to be disregarded as visionary and impossible of attainment? Before joining in that judgment, it will be well to recall the words which that hard-headed businessman and corporation lawyer, Wendell Willkie, wrote after he had come up against the realities of Asia.

" The temptation is great, in all of us," said Mr. Willkie, " to limit the objectives of a war. Cynically, we may hope that the big words we have used will become smaller at the peace table, and that we can avoid the costly and difficult readjustments which will be required to establish and defend real freedom for all peoples."

Then Mr. Willkie went on, with the aid of specific illustrations, to show how literally the colonial peoples have taken our " big words " about freedom, and how necessary it is that, in the making of peace, we do something commensurate with those expectations.

" The world is awake at last," he continued, " to the knowledge that the rule of people by other peoples is not freedom, and not what we must fight to preserve. There will be lots of tough problems ahead. And they will differ in different mandates and different colonies. Not all the peoples of the world are ready for freedom, or can defend it, the day after tomorrow. But today they all want some date to work toward, some assurance that the date will be kept. For the future, they do not ask that we solve their problems for them. They are neither so foolish nor so fainthearted. They ask only for the chance to solve their own problems with economic as well as political cooperation. For the peoples of the world intend to be free not only for their political satisfaction, but also for their economic advancement." [3]

" Some date to work toward, some assurance that the date will be kept." World peace cannot exist for long if the billion inhabitants of the colonial territories become convinced that they are being denied justice, that the white minority intends

[3] From *One World*, by Wendell L. Willkie. New York: Simon and Schuster, 1943. Quoted by permission.

to hold them in a subjection which will last for generations or centuries. They will plot, they will sabotage, they will revolt, they will use any available weapon and measure to produce chaos, in the despairing hope that out of chaos there may emerge a better fate. If the colonial system is to be continued at all, the only way in which to continue it with the free consent and peaceful cooperation of the colonial peoples is by holding before them just such a promise of future liberty as Mr. Willkie has seen is required: "Some date to work toward, some assurance that the date will be kept."

This, in spirit and in its main proposal, is essentially the same program for the liquidation of empires as that which the Christian church put forward at Delaware. The time has come, in every colonial territory on earth, to open a straight road to freedom, to set a definite goal toward which every freedom-seeking people can work and toward which the administration of every colony shall be directed, and to provide firm guarantees that the promises made will be kept when the conditions laid down have been fulfilled.

It should occasion no surprise that the church, with its unmatched sources of information through its missionary enterprises in Asia, Africa and the islands of the sea, and this American political leader, who was not content to rely on second-hand reports but went to see Africa and Asia for himself, should have come to the same conclusions. Given the facts of world-wide revolt against the perpetuation of imperialism, given a readiness to face these facts without the bias of an itch for empire, and the resulting recommendations could not but be closely akin. Since they are so nearly in accord, however, let no man seek to escape the prophetic insight of the church's proposals by traducing them as visionary or impracticable. Like all prophetic truth, they represent the sternest realism.

Three Footnotes on the Future of Empires

I.

In some respects, the most disquieting element in the problem of imperialism is the growth of an imperialistic tendency in the United States. Before the present war signs were multiplying that the United States was about to reduce its colonial responsibilities. Pressure from agricultural interests had resulted in the adoption of the Tydings-McDuffie Act, which promised full independence to the Philippines on July 4, 1946. Agitation was growing for some action in the Caribbean which would grant genuine self-government to Puerto Rico, just as the repeal of the Platt Amendment in the early days of the Roosevelt administration had given full liberty to Cuba. The campaign to release Hawaii from its anomalous status — half autonomous territory, half naval reservation — by granting full statehood had gained impressive proportions.

Today the tide is running in the other direction. Secretary Knox's declaration in favor of obtaining naval bases in all parts of the Pacific as part of the spoils of war undoubtedly has large public support. Thus, a poll published by *Fortune* in June 1943 shows that in answer to the question, " Do you think the United States should come out of the war with more military bases outside this country than we had before the war? " 84 per cent of those answering said Yes, 8.1 per cent said No, and 7.9 per cent expressed themselves as undecided. Growing appreciation of the prospective instability of the world situation, regardless of the war's outcome, and a vague but widespread feeling that the United States should use its great power to impose order, has apparently persuaded a large part of the American public that after the war the Stars and Stripes should be kept afloat over strategic spots throughout the world. The establishment of American bases as a war measure in British and Dutch possessions in the western Atlantic and Caribbean, as well as in a few South American countries, has given birth to an expectation that these bases will be maintained indefinitely. (The destroyer deal with the British provided for 99-year leases for the American bases established on eight British colonies.) There is considerable discussion of the advantage of acquiring permanent American bases in the Azores and either at Dakar in West Africa or in that immediate vicinity.

There is no partisan cast to these demands for enormous expansion of American territorial holdings for "defense" purposes. They are quite as likely to come from Republicans as from Democrats. Thus, on August 26, 1943, the former executive director of the Republican National Committee, Clarence Budington Kelland, made public the postwar blueprint which he planned to submit to a September meeting of the Republican Postwar Policy Committee. In prewar days Mr. Kelland was generally lumped among the isolationists. Today he speaks in this fashion:

We are reluctant to extend our borders, but at last we must face realities, respond to no wave of mawkish sentimentality, no silly surge of renunciation or unselfishness. We must at last be selfish, with the future, the impregnability of our country, clearly in mind. We must take what we must have. And we must have such spots on the surface of the earth as will ring this land with a mighty circle of Gibraltars through whose cordon no enemy can ever penetrate with invading army or fleet to reach our shores.

As our . . . final zone of safety we must possess, by friendly negotiation if we may, by occupation if we must, those points, those islands, those bases which will perfect the fortification of the United States. The islands of the Pacific, in what number and in what location are essential to us, must become ours to have and to hold. The Pacific Ocean must become an American lake . . . to guarantee that there can never be another Pearl Harbor. . . .

We must not content ourselves with fortifying the Pacific. We must turn to the Atlantic, and there again we must acquire by treaty or by occupation such islands, such territories as we deem necessary to our safety.[4]

" No silly surge of unselfishness." " We must take what we must have." Behold the American Empire!

Moreover, in quarters which would reject proposals for the projection of any such program of political imperialism, there is a noticeable readiness to play with the idea of an American postwar economic empire. The argument is that the American capitalistic economy must acquire a vast multiplication of overseas outlets in order to operate without mass unemployment, that opportunities for such economic expansion will beckon from all parts of the globe after the war, and that only the United States will have the financial and manufacturing resources to take full advantage of these opportunities. Hence arise the expectations of an " American Century," and similar ideas. Such a thoughtful Asiatic leader as Jawaharlal Nehru has already expressed his fear that American economic imperialism will thus attempt to fasten controls on what have been colonial regions even more complete than have been the controls of the political imperialism of the past.

It is highly necessary that the American people as a whole shall be brought to understand the imperialistic realities behind all such proposals, both political and economic. They must be made to reckon the cost, not only in the maintenance of the armed forces which would be required, but in the growth of ill will among the peoples who are determined to achieve freedom.

One reassuring sign that the rise of this spirit of imperialism has not overwhelmed the American government is to be found in the specific promise made to President Quezon by President Roosevelt that the United States will make good on its pledge to grant the Philippines full independence in 1946, and that it

[4] As quoted in the *New York Times*, August 26, 1943.

will seek international guarantees for the future integrity of the Philippine Republic.

2.

Any American writing on the future of imperialism will speak with caution and humility on the subject of India, especially since our own colonial record in Puerto Rico and the Virgin Islands has been so poor. Nevertheless, Mr. Willkie was undoubtedly correct when he said that, in judging the intentions of the West toward Eastern aspirations for liberty, the key question throughout the Orient has become: What about India? [5] Until something of a definitive nature is done about India, Mr. Wallace may continue to proclaim that in the postwar world " no nation will have the God-given right to exploit other nations," and Mr. Welles that " the age of imperialism is ended," and the subject peoples will set the words down as more examples of the incurable hypocrisy of the ruling white.

Because of the enforced quiet in India, where, Mr. Churchill states, more white soldiers are now stationed than at any previous time in its history, many apparently think that the problem of India has been solved. It is not so. There will probably be no uprisings in India while the war continues; almost certainly there will be none if there is no Japanese invasion — a now remote possibility. But Britain cannot go on ruling India indefinitely by a process of jailing thousands of her leaders. Liberal opinion in England, if no other factor, will eventually sicken of such a colonial policy and force a change.

It must be remembered, in addition, that two factors within India are to change soon. In the first place, the war will end. That will free millions of Indians from their fear lest a policy of nationalistic agitation play into the hands of Japanese imperialism. The extent to which Indian nationalists have re-

[5] Cf. *One World*, p. 76.

frained from full-scale revolt because of this Japanese menace will probably become apparent as soon as the war in the Pacific ends. In the second place, nationalist leadership will pass from the hands of Mr. Gandhi. Mr. Gandhi will die, probably to be succeeded by Mr. Nehru. In any event, leadership of the nationalist movement will no longer be committed to non-violence. Revolutionary agitation will therefore increasingly resort to measures which Mr. Gandhi has eschewed and denounced.

Nor should it be overlooked that, with the close of the war, pressure for a grant of freedom to India will be renewed from other Asiatic quarters. Chiang Kai-shek has already gone to considerable lengths to show China's sympathy for Indian aspirations and his own personal friendship for Mr. Nehru. This Chinese agitation has died down in recent months, owing to the exigencies of the war and China's own hope for help from armies operating from an Indian base. But it will surely be renewed after the defeat of Japan, and it will be of considerable potency in keeping the Asiatic caldron bubbling. At the same time, Russia is likely to find many ways of making clear its sympathy for the Indian nationalists and of encouraging the independence movement within India. Considerable significance attaches to the recent proportionately rapid growth of the Communist party in India.

What, then, should Britain do with regard to India? Renew the offer of dominion status contained in the Cripps proposal? That offer, it has been officially announced, still stands and is the only offer which Britain is prepared to make. Let India take it or leave it! Many who wish to see India obtain self-government believe that the Cripps proposal offered self-government and that India should take it. But E. Stanley Jones, who is probably the most widely known Christian missionary in India, shows how the Cripps offer looks from the Indian standpoint:

What was Britain's offer? To grant dominion status while reserving defense. In essence, Britain said: "You can govern yourself but you cannot defend yourself." India could not take self-government on a spearpoint of domination. . . . To reserve "defense" meant that about 75 per cent of the revenues of India would be in British hands — for approximately that amount goes for the military. Thus about 25 per cent would be left the Indians with which to begin self-government. How could India begin self-government with only 25 per cent of its revenues under its control? Is that an offer of self-government? Let Japan offer the whites the return of Malaya on those terms, and see what they would say! And yet responsible men continue to declare that self-government was offered India and India would not take it.[6]

Something must be done at the war's close to convince India that it is to be granted genuine freedom. As Dr. Jones goes on to point out in the article from which I have just quoted, the root problem is that Indians of all classes have no faith in British intentions. They believe that after the last war England failed to fulfill promises which, however ambiguously worded, were understood to pledge rapid postwar progress toward self-government, and they have no faith that the same thing will not happen again, whatever promises may be made under the stress of war. Other Asiatics, it is to be feared, share the same skepticism. That it is not irrational is suggested by the debate which continues even in Britain as to how much the British government is actually pledged to grant India in the way of self-government after the war. Such an English journalist as H. N. Brailsford constantly reveals that he does not believe there are any binding pledges of importance. And the poised correspondent of the *New York Times*, Herbert L. Matthews, allowed the same note of skepticism to creep into the article which he wrote at the close of a year's study of the situation.

[6] From an article, "Sponges on Spearpoints," in the *Christian Century* for August 25, 1943. Quoted by permission.

In his review, Mr. Matthews paid generous tribute to the British administration of India and severely criticized many claims of the Indian National Congress to represent Indian sentiment. Nevertheless, a careful reading will show that he also, after studying the problem with a care equaled by few Americans, does not believe that there is convincing evidence that Britain intends to grant India self-government at any time in the foreseeable future.

The difficulty here, it would appear, lies in the moral realm. Without a conviction of good faith it is unlikely that any solution can be found for the India problem which will leave that subcontinent other stability than the stability of a prison-yard. Hence the churches of Great Britain have a remarkable opportunity and responsibility. It is the opportunity to seek means for the reopening of negotiations between the British government and the leaders of all the important parties and communal groups of India. (All of them, incidentally, rejected the Cripps proposal.) It is the responsibility to see that, whatever future offer the British government may make, it is couched in such terms and accompanied by such guarantees that there can be no continuing question as to British good faith or the determination of Britain to perform whatever she may agree.

Fortunately, British churchmen appear to be awakening to this responsibility and opportunity. As might be expected, this awakening is coming first among Christian missionaries in India itself. While the government maintains its adamant stand, while the appointment of Field Marshal Wavell as viceroy shows that it intends to continue to rule with a strong hand, twenty-five British missionaries have urged that the necessity for reopening the whole question of self-government be recognized, that as a preliminary for renewed discussions the government grant amnesty " to all political prisoners not convicted of crimes of violence who are prepared to follow constitutional methods," and that after these nationalist leaders have been released from prison the government provide that the representative body proposed in the Cripps plan be called into existence, to begin work at once on the writing of a new constitution. Among the signers of this remarkable document are the Anglican bishops of Calcutta and Madras, and representatives of the London, Baptist and Methodist missionary societies, the Church of Scotland mission, the National Christian Council of India and the Cambridge mission.

At the same time, the British Council of Churches has sent a message to the National Christian Council of India deploring the political deadlock, admitting a share of British responsibility for a " soreness and alienation deeply rooted in history, whose ultimate causes are moral and spiritual," and pledging to do its full part in inaugurating and carrying through a new work of reconciliation. It may well be that the Christian church is herewith entering on a prophetic mission in relation to one of the most involved and baffling political problems in the contemporary world.

3

The Atlantic Charter opens with a pledge that its signatories " seek no aggrandizement, territorial or other." Similar declarations pledging " no annexations and no indemnities " were made during the first World War. Yet various states of the victorious Allies came out of that war with 1,100,000 square miles of territory taken from Germany, most of it in the form of mandates which sought to disguise the fact of appropriation. Great Britain and her dominions got by far the lion's share of this haul; France and Japan each received important shares. Italy got nothing, which helps to explain why she changed sides for the second World War.

One need not believe that the United Nations are consciously " seeking " territorial gains to foresee the possibility that such gains may accrue to certain of them as a means of strengthening their military security in case of another general war. On July 15, 1943, for example, Major Clement R. Attlee, leader of the Labor party and deputy to Mr. Churchill in Parliament, told the House of Commons that the Atlantic Charter is not to be construed as making it impossible for the United Nations to retain any key territory captured in the war which they consider necessary to the preservation of peace. According to the press, Parliament broke into loud cheers at the assurance. The political finesse with which Mr. Churchill thus placed the responsibility for the official announcement of this significant further "interpretation" of the Atlantic Charter on the leader of the Labor party, must be acknowledged.

The threat to the future contained in such a statement as that by Major Attlee cannot be denied. It is nonsense to proclaim the end of imperialism and at the same time to occupy Ethiopia, Eritrea, North Africa or the islands of the Pacific under an extension of the doctrine of military necessity into time of peace. If the war should be followed by any such widespread acquisition of territory in the name of military security, then it must be realized that the old imperialistic order is still functioning at full strength and toward its often demonstrated result — war.

CHAPTER VI

THE RACE DEMON

I

No issue threatens the durability of the coming peace as does that of race. If the postwar world cannot work out some means of recognizing the equality of races, if certain parts of the white world persist in acting as though pigmentation gave them an inherent right to demand deference from all the tinted peoples, there is nothing ahead but trouble. As one who has had some slight contact with that portion of the world which is demanding freedom from Western domination, I can testify that there is no other single factor which is working with equal power to produce so ghastly a crisis in human affairs. The Orient is determined to put an end to what it regards as the racial arrogance of the Occident. If the Occident fails to read correctly the signs of the times, and to revise its racial habits in the light thereof, it is quite conceivable that the third World War will be, in the main, a race war. World war between the races would make the wars we have so far suffered pale into insignificance alongside its ruthlessness and savagery.

Few realize how modern is the race issue in its present form. Yet it is only ninety years since the Frenchman, Count Gobineau, published his four-volume tome, *Essai sur l'inégalité des races humaines,* and so gave most of our modern racial superstitions a pseudo-scientific foundation. Pigmentation, Gobineau claimed, determines mental and spiritual differences between men. "Mixture of blood" produces degeneracy, and is responsible for the decline and fall of civilizations. A straight line runs from the racial fancies of this erstwhile French diplo-

mat to the Aryan theories of that Englishman-turned-German,
Houston Stewart Chamberlain, which have reached their crud-
est expression and glorification in the bigotry of the Ku Klux
Klan in America and the racial insanity of Hitler and his Nazis
in Germany.

But the racial question first took the spotlight on the international stage at the Paris Peace Conference in 1919. There
for the first time in a gathering of the major nations the Japanese delegation brought the race issue into the open and tried to
force the other powers to face and deal with it. In so doing,
the Japanese insisted that their purpose was simply to secure a
general declaration of racial equality which would satisfy the
pride of the Oriental peoples and so remove this from the list
of questions which might, in the future, exacerbate the relations between Eastern and Western nations. There is no reason to doubt the sincerity of this Japanese explanation. But if
that was the purpose which the delegates from the Orient had
in view, they received a rude setback. The conference refused to allow any recognition of racial equality, even of the
vaguest and most inferential nature, to go into the Covenant of
the League of Nations which it was creating. And the two
delegations which blocked any such recognition were those of
the United States and Great Britain.

Because of the historic consequences which have flowed
from the rebuff administered to Japanese racial sensibilities at
Paris, it is worth recalling in some detail what happened there.
The story has been told several times; most of the many memoirs written by participants in the conference attempt some
explanation or justification of the treatment of the racial issue.
But no account surpasses in accuracy and objectivity that contained in the book, *Versailles Twenty Years After*, written by
the professor of history at Williams College, Dr. Paul Birdsall.
I shall follow closely, therefore, Professor Birdsall's record in
attempting to refresh the minds of my readers as to the way in

which the race question became an international issue at the peace conference which ended the previous World War.

II

On the insistence of President Wilson, the Paris Peace Conference made the writing of the Covenant of the proposed League of Nations the first matter on its agenda. The commission to carry out this task, under the chairmanship of the American President, completed its draft of that document on February 13. At that time there was an Article XXI in the Covenant affirming religious equality. The Japanese member of the commission, Baron Makino, accordingly offered an amendment to that article:

The equality of nations being a basic principle of the League of Nations, the High Contracting Parties agree to accord, as soon as possible, to all alien nationals of states members of the League, equal and just treatment in every respect, making no distinction, either in law or fact, on account of their race or nationality.

Baron Makino, says Dr. Birdsall, " disclaimed any intention of requiring immediate and complete realization of the principle in all its details. He fully recognized that the question of race prejudice was a very delicate and complicated matter. He would ask the adoption of his clause as an enunciation of principle and ' an invitation to the governments and peoples concerned to examine the question more seriously and closely, and to devise some acceptable means to meet a deadlock which at present confronts different peoples.' " [1]

Despite the Japanese explanation, Lord Robert Cecil, on behalf of the British delegation, blocked the adoption of the amendment, saying that it raised " extremely serious problems

---

[1] From *Versailles Twenty Years After*, by Paul Birdsall. New York: Reynal & Hitchcock, 1941. Quoted by permission, as are also the other quotations in this chapter taken from the same book.

within the British Empire." Thereupon Colonel House withdrew Article XXI entirely.

The next day President Wilson sailed for the United States. There, during a month of conferences, he discovered that in order to hope for ratification of American adherence to the League by the Senate, he would be forced to reopen the question of amending the Covenant, on his return to Paris, in order to insert a specific exemption of all matters of domestic legislation from the purview of the League. But to reopen the matter of the text of the Covenant meant that Japan would be given an opportunity to renew her motion for an amendment in some degree recognizing racial equality. President Wilson and his advisers hated to do it, but the intransigence of the Senate had left them no choice. To placate the Senate, they had to give Japan her second chance.

Meanwhile, the pot boiled behind the scenes in Paris. All sorts of unofficial negotiations went on between the principal delegations, trying to work out some form of statement on the race issue which would satisfy the Orientals (for China had associated itself with Japan in seeking a recognition of racial equality) and yet would not make trouble in the " white supremacy " nations. Every effort to formulate a compromise declaration came to grief, however, on the adamant opposition of Premier Hughes of Australia, who was acting as a member of the British delegation. It was Hughes, incidentally, far more than Clemenceau or any other delegate, who sought to block and deride the efforts of President Wilson at almost every stage of the conference. Writes Birdsall:

Hughes made it clear to his British colleagues that if they and the Americans agreed even to the mildest formula of racial equality, he would publicly raise the whole question at a plenary session of the peace conference. He threatened to appeal deliberately to the racial prejudices of the Dominions and the United States, to " raise a storm of protest not only in the Dominions but in the western part of the United States." Lord Robert Cecil, General Smuts and Colonel House did not dare run that risk.

That last sentence of Dr. Birdsall's speaks volumes as to the real nature of the race problem. It is easy, on the basis of the official records of the Paris gathering, to present Premier Hughes as the villain in the race drama. But Mr. Hughes would have been powerless had he not known that he could rely for support on the racial feeling of all the Dominions and of millions of Americans. That racial feeling is just as strong today as in 1919; perhaps stronger.

The race issue came to a climax on April 11 when the commission to write the League Covenant held its last session. Both Colonel House and Lord Robert Cecil begged the Japanese not to bring the question up again, but without success. Let Birdsall tell what happened:

All that Makino asked was the insertion in the preamble to the Covenant of the simple words: ". . . by the endorsement of the principles of the equality of nations and just treatment of their nationals." The dangerous word 'race' did not appear, and the principle itself was the merest generality of the most harmless kind, separated entirely from the specific provisions of the body of the Covenant itself. If there remained the slightest chance that it could be interpreted to affect immigration policies, that danger was entirely removed by adoption of the American amendment which removed such questions from the competence of the League. Makino said that he had no intention that his amendment "encroach on the internal affairs of any nation." It fell far short of Japanese desires, but it was an honest attempt to compose differences of viewpoint.

Cecil, whose hands were tied, made a pathetic speech. He personally agreed with the Japanese proposal, but "regretted that he was not in a position to vote for this amendment." The rest of his speech was a deliberate evasion of the issue. In effect, he said that any race clause adopted by the commission was bound to encroach upon the sovereignty of states. He thereupon stated

the profound truth that either the Japanese proposal meant something, or it did not. If it had legal effect it was unacceptable. He
left it at that, without ever meeting the Japanese offer to accept
what they admitted was meaningless for the sake of prestige and
to satisfy the people at home. The recorded words of the speech
betray perplexity and embarrassment, and David Hunter Miller,
who heard it, says that after Cecil spoke he looked fixedly at the
table in front of him without ever once raising his eyes.

President Wilson, according to Dr. Birdsall, wanted to accept this amendment, but Colonel House warned him that to
do so " would raise the race issue throughout the world." So
the American President warned the commission that the amendment would, if adopted, make trouble, and put the vote.
Eleven delegations voted in the affirmative; none in the negative. But President Wilson, as chairman, ruled that the amendment required unanimous approval by all the delegations represented on the commission, and since two — the British and
the American — had refrained from voting, he declared the
amendment lost.

It was still feared that the Japanese might press their amendment at the plenary session of the entire peace conference,
which was held seventeen days later formally to adopt the Covenant and bring the League of Nations into being. They had
a parliamentary right to do so. If they had, they would have
placed the United States and Great Britain on public record
in most embarrassing fashion as denying the principle of equality between races and between members of the League. Baron
Makino did, in fact, make a speech at the plenary session and
seemed for a time to be leading up to a renewal of the demand
for adoption of the original Japanese amendment. It is not
difficult to imagine the uncomfortable feelings of the British
and American delegates as Makino went on, or the sardonic
gleam in Clemenceau's eye as he surveyed his Anglo-American
colleagues, whose claims to moral virtue in the intricacies of

international negotiation caused him such acute disgust. But Baron Makino, after talking right up to the point of actually moving the racial equality amendment, veered away, and left his colleagues congratulating themselves on their narrow escape. It was, as Birdsall says, simply a closing speech for the record. But what a record!

III

I have recounted that story at such length because the race issue, as an international source of friction, has been growing ever since the Paris Peace Conference. Close observers of the Orient — and some in Africa — have been warning the West throughout the last twenty years of the rapid rise of racial self-consciousness and pride among the tinted peoples. And the whites living in Asia and Africa, it must be admitted, have done little to assuage the racial sensibilities of the native inhabitants. On the contrary, many of them have conducted themselves as though it was their purpose to make all yellow, brown and black men hate the sight of a white. Almost the only exception has been in the case of Christian missionaries.

In the port cities of China, across the length and breadth of India, in Manila and Singapore and Batavia, and everywhere throughout Central and South Africa, white military and business communities have insisted on social rules of racial segregation which have daily flung the racial challenge full into the faces of the native population. There is some debate as to whether the parks of Shanghai, for instance, ever actually displayed signs reading, "No dogs or Chinese allowed." But there can be no dispute as to the fact that Chinese (except nurses in charge of white children) were excluded from the Shanghai parks. Nor that highly educated Chinese, many of them possessing advanced degrees from British and American universities, found themselves excluded from the British and American clubs in that city. The racial bar was maintained with equal rigidity against Filipinos in the American officers' club in Manila. As to the racial laws in South Africa, and the white opinion which insists upon them and sees that they are enforced, one can only say that they are probably preparing the way for the most tragic racial conflict the world has ever seen.

Probably no American knows the realities of this racial tension as it exists in the Far East better than Pearl S. Buck, who wrote *The Good Earth* and is one of the two Americans who have received the Nobel prize in literature. Mrs. Buck is devoting almost all her powers these days to rouse her fellow Americans, and Westerners in general, to a realization of the need for some generous and far-reaching action to tear down walls of racial separation. Typical of the words of warning which she has uttered again and again are these:

It is worse than folly — it is dangerous today — not to recognize the truth, for in it lies the tinder for tomorrow. Who of us can doubt it who has seen a white policeman beat a Chinese coolie in Shanghai, . . . an English captain lash out with his whip at an Indian vender? Who of us, having seen such Oriental sights or heard the common contemptuous talk of the white man in any colored country, can forget the fearful, bitter hatred in the colored face and the blaze in the dark eyes? Who of us can be so stupid as not to see the future written there? The most dangerous human stupidity has been that of the white race in the baseless prejudice through which even the meanest of white creatures has felt he could despise a king if his skin was dark. . . . The deep patience of colored peoples is at an end. Everywhere among them there is the same resolve for freedom and equality that white Americans and British have; but it is a grimmer resolve, for it includes the determination to be rid of white rule and exploitation and white race prejudice, and nothing will weaken this will.[2]

[2] From *American Unity and Asia,* by Pearl S. Buck. New York: The John Day Company, Inc. Quoted by permission.

Mrs. Buck has put her finger fairly on one of the root causes of misunderstanding between East and West. Back of the racial sensitiveness of Orientals today lies a sorry record of personal insult at the hands of boorish whites. Talk, for example, with an Indian nationalist about his reasons for demanding independence and you will find, in almost every instance, if you probe far enough, that after he has listed the familiar catalogue of Britain's shortcomings in colonial administration, he will tell at last of some personal experience when a white has presumed on his racial status to force the Indian into inferior quarters in a railway train or to debar him from some social occasion. It is then, to use again Mrs. Buck's descriptive words, that the " fearful, bitter hatred " flames in the colored face and blazes from the dark eyes.

Even some of our Western proposals for a postwar order which we regard as idealistic appear to thoughtful Orientals tainted with racial snobbery. Thus the famous Chinese scholar, Lin Yutang, writes:

In spite of the failure of white leadership this racial arrogance, of which we accuse Hitler and Göbbels, still persists. In the East it exists in the form of just bad manners. In the West it comes out in many curious forms among the most intelligent, educated circles such as the Clarence Streit idea of Anglo-American mastery of the world and general unwillingness to define a new world charter and face the issues of colonies. I believe the idea of Anglo-American mastery of the world is potentially very strong and effective and will be so at the peace conference.[3]

Mr. Willkie believes that the war has already taught Westerners the baselessness of their racial prejudices and assumptions of superiority.[4] The Chinese philosopher, as his latest book, *Between Tears and Laughter*, shows, believes that we have scarcely begun to learn that lesson. Which is right?

[3] Quoted by permission of the author.
[4] Cf. *One World*, p. 79.

The Japanese are fighting this war under a slogan, "Asia for the Asiatics." We sneer at that slogan as an obvious propaganda trick. When they march into Thailand, Malaya, Burma, Indonesia and the Philippines proclaiming that they come to free the inhabitants from white rule, we recall their bloody record in Korea, Manchuria and central China and ask who can be fooled by such a pretense. When Premier Tojo grants 'independence' to Burma and restores territory to Thailand, we point out the empty nature of such gestures at this stage of the war. Nevertheless, in their "Asia for the Asiatics" slogan the Japanese have coined a watchword which, whatever their own fate in this war, will not be forgotten. It expresses an aspiration to which the racial pretensions of the white man in the Far East have given passionate meaning all the way from Bagdad to Tokyo. And when the Japanese propagandists taunt such Asiatics as are ready to ally themselves with us with the claim that they are joining hands with those who still display racial arrogance, who still claim an innate superiority, what are we to say?

IV

The racial issue did not die at the Paris Peace Conference. It is coming up again when the treaties are written at the close of this war. Last time it was the Japanese who brought it up. This time it will be the Chinese and the Filipinos and the Indonesians. Indeed, the issue is already up so far as the United States is concerned in the existence of the legislation which forbids admission of Asiatics to this country or their eligibility for American citizenship.

Of course, the United States is not alone in raising such racial bars. Similar legislation excludes Asiatics from Canada, Australia, New Zealand and the Union of South Africa. So far as legal status is concerned, these are the nations which share with Nazi Germany the dubious distinction of having written racial discrimination into their statutes.

Does anything strike you about this list of countries where the racial bar is a matter of law — Germany, Canada, Australia, New Zealand, the Union of South Africa, the United States? Perhaps the fact has no special significance, but it is worth noting that these are all dominantly Protestant states and that, with the exception of Germany, they are given to boast of their leadership as democracies. Where do their racial policies leave their moral pretensions?

In answer to that question, let us call again upon the testimony of a source entirely outside the church and hardly to be suspected of excessive idealistic or humanitarian tendencies. *Fortune*, that magazine which almost automatically limits its circulation to the wealthy with its $10-a-year subscription price, not long ago fell to discussing American racial policy, as exemplified in Chinese exclusion. Here is a part of what it had to say:

It may surprise many of our citizens to know that Congress long ago anticipated and wrote into the law a fundamental theory of Adolf Hitler's race theology. . . . To continue such laws and attitudes in the face of our avowed aims is to make the aims ridiculous and their avowal contemptible. The Japanese have been quick to point out to all Asia our evident hypocrisy; and so far the only answer we have made, or can make, is to change the subject. . . . We should conclude at once an immigration and naturalization treaty with China, providing for the reciprocal admission of certain classes, such as merchants and intellectuals, and making eligible for naturalization all those admitted to permanent residence. . . . This change in American immigration law, like the proposed changes in our tariff, are, or will be, measures of expediency. We recommend them because they are indisputably to our eventual interest, in so far as experience and reason can show us what our future interest is.

In defining our aims in Asia we have made use of large-sounding terms. We have called our great ends in view, human dignity and freedom. Large-sounding terms and great ends are readily forthcoming when nations at war seek to justify their resort to a use of force condemned by their intelligence, their morality and their religion. This joint condemnation is a heavy load for the rational man to bear while he does the ugly and ignoble things that he sees and knows he must do in sheer defense of his rationality, his right to hope, and his right to be free. It is more than ever incumbent on us, when in this necessity we hate those who hate us and, far from doing good to them, are unalterably resolved to pay back with a devastating despite those who despitefully use us, to maintain in every way we can the principles embodied in our ultimate aims. We must translate our high-sounding terms into everyday measures of immigration policy and tariff law if we are not ready to admit that our enemies are, in part at least, right about us.[5]

Yet despite this clear perception of the need for immediate action to clear up the position of the United States on the racial issue, nothing has so far been done and it begins to look increasingly probable that nothing will be done. In response to the popular acclaim accorded Madame Chiang Kai-shek at the time of her visit to this country, about half a dozen bills and resolutions were introduced into Congress, all with the intention of lifting the exclusion laws which now specifically debar Chinese from admission into the United States and applying to them the same quota principle of admission which, since 1924, has ruled the admission of immigrants from outside the so-called " Asiatic barred zone." (Enactment of such legislation would not increase by a single person the total of 150,000 immigrants a year now eligible for admission; the Chinese quota, under such an amendment of the law, would be 106 or 107

[5] From a supplement, " The United States in a New World. II: Pacific Relations," published in *Fortune*, August 1942. Copyright by Time, Inc., and quoted by permission.

admissions a year — hardly the " inundating yellow wave " that demagogues on the Pacific coast howl about.) But not one of these bills has been acted upon by the immigration committee of the House of Representatives, much less reported out to the floor of Congress.

Nor does that tell the whole dismal story. Any thoughtful person will see that legislation which simply lifts the bars now holding out Chinese will not clear up the record of the United States on the issue of race discrimination. It will still leave in effect the rest of that considerable body of legislation, regulations and judicial decisions which debars other Asiatics.[6] It is certain, therefore, to be regarded generally in Asia as simply a sop flung to a dissatisfied ally, a bribe expediently passed to keep the vital Chinese front in being until we are able to turn our whole attention to the war in the Pacific. Yet not only are those members of Congress who are most eager to see all marks of racial discrimination wiped from our statutes unanimously of the opinion that it would be impossible at this time to introduce such legislation with the slightest hope of success, but some whose judgment carries great weight believe that if even a bill confining the effort to do racial justice to the Chinese should reach the floor, it will be seized on by some Congressmen as a pretext for an outburst of racial vituperation which will do irreparable damage to America's standing with the peoples of the East.

V

Moreover, our racial problem at home immensely complicates our dealing with peoples of other races overseas. Mr.

[6] Interestingly enough, the racial exclusion laws do not keep Negroes out of the United States. The reason simply is that the naturalization laws were amended in 1870, at the time when Congress was trying to force southern states to adopt constitutions doing away with racial discrimination, to allow the naturalization of " aliens of African nativity " and " persons of African descent." The eligibility of Negroes for admission and citizenship is therefore to be included among the results of the Civil War.

Willkie, when once he had achieved the vantage-point of Chungking, saw this clearly. " The attitude of the white citizens of this country toward the Negroes," he wrote, " has undeniably had some of the unlovely characteristics of an alien imperialism — a smug racial superiority, a willingness to exploit an unprotected people. . . . Our very proclamations of what we are fighting for have rendered our own inequities self-evident. When we talk of freedom and opportunity for all nations, the mocking paradoxes in our own society become so clear they can no longer be ignored. If we want to talk about freedom, we must mean freedom for others as well as ourselves, and we must mean freedom for everyone inside our frontiers as well as outside." [7]

It is revealing to see how, in seeking a cheap and easy method to round up votes, certain demagogues on the Pacific coast are today resorting to the white supremacy issue in exactly the same way demagogues in the South have employed it for years. It would be hard to think of any development with more potentiality of future catastrophe for the Republic than to have two great sections in which political success, with access to the spoils of office, should depend on success in stirring up racial animosities. The one-party, one-dominant-issue South already constitutes a sadly indigestible lump in our democratic experiment. Add another such sectional region denying this fundamental postulate of democracy, and the experiment would be all but doomed.

I do not intend to discuss the race issue inside the United States at any length. But its existence must be acknowledged in any consideration of the problems of the postwar order. And despite all the efforts which devoted men and women on both sides of the racial line are making to assuage the bitterness of the white and Negro masses, I believe that a candid appraisal of the situation will lead to the conclusion that racial

[7] From *One World*, p. 79.

tension inside the United States is not decreasing, but is growing. I know that my own acquaintances who are closest to the question, in both South and North, are increasingly apprehensive as to the future.

It seems to me silly to try to deny that there is a growing bitterness, both among Negroes and among those whites who feel their economic security most menaced by the demand of Negroes for more and better jobs. Despite all that the President and his subordinates have done to provide more work for Negroes in war industries, the Negroes feel that they are still denied access to jobs and wage scales for which they are fitted. They feel that they have been the last to be hired, that they are still discriminated against in matters of union membership, promotion and seniority rights, and that when the war ends they will be the first to be fired. On the other hand, there are plenty of brooding whites — and not all of them in the South, by any means — who will tell you on the slightest provocation that one of the first jobs in which they intend to have a part after the war is to " put the uppity niggers in their place."

On the whole, the tension is probably felt more deeply on the Negro's side of the line. Negroes are particularly bitter about the discriminatory treatment which, they allege, has been given members of their race in the armed forces of the United States. That is why the riots in Harlem, the Negro district in New York, in midsummer 1943, were of even greater significance than those in Detroit. No overt clash between the races occurred to touch off the Harlem spark, but when a rumor swept through the district that a Negro soldier had been mistreated by a policeman in the presence of the soldier's mother, the wild outburst started which led to five deaths and widespread rioting. In other words, the mere rumor that another black man in uniform had suffered injury was enough to topple the largest Negro population center in the country into frenzied disorder.

As some indication of this racial tension as it is felt within America's armed forces, I am going to take the liberty of reproducing one paragraph from a letter just received from a Negro chaplain stationed in an army training center in the United States where most of the troops are Negroes:

When men are segregated because of their color, abused, and denied, what kind of message has the chaplain for them? When men come to you discouraged and demoralized because of the brutal treatment accorded their parents and loved ones at home, what can you tell them about the reasons why they fight? When soldiers of your unit go on furloughs and suffer abuses that would make Hitler frown, what kind of balm are you going to give their troubled souls? If these men were not told that they were training to engage an enemy bent on destroying their liberties, maybe the pill would not be so hard to swallow. But the chaplain is supposed to keep the spirit alive in men while at the same time it is being crushed every day by their fellow Americans. I tell you there are times when, like Jeremiah of old, we cry, "O that my head were water and mine eyes a fountain of tears, that I might cry night and day for the slain daughter of my people."

One is tempted to reproduce quotations from the Negro press of a far more embittered and inflammatory nature.

VI

There is an understandable tendency in governmental circles in the United States and Great Britain to gloss over or attempt to ignore the relation of this issue to the making of a durable peace. If the race demon could cause so much discord at Paris a quarter-century ago, what catastrophe might befall if it were allowed to run at large today? The result is an effort to evade, to discourage discussion, to place the blame for continued reference to racial tensions on "agitators," "fifth columnists," "Nazi-Jap agents."

In the long run, such a policy will only produce an explosion,

or series of explosions, which will shake the world. Thoughtful leaders of government must know this. But they feel helpless in the absence of a constructive governmental race policy.
And they insist that there can be no such policy while the governments of the United States, Britain and the Dominions are
dependent on votes, while votes are swayed by race prejudice,
and while even such a timid step toward racial justice as repeal
of the Chinese exclusion laws would produce a legislative crisis.

In the presence of such official cowardice, surely the Christian church has a duty to discharge. It must proclaim the
truth about the race issue as it now divides the peoples and
threatens to bring them into eventual and appalling conflict.
It must point the way by which the nations, both in their international relations and in their domestic affairs, may reach
the security of mutual racial respect and understanding. And
it must insist, with a persistence which neither governments
nor peoples can continue to ignore, that until this demon of
racial antagonism is exorcised there can be no lasting peace, no
general justice, no freedom from fear.

The Delaware Conference was notable for the courage with
which, speaking as the voice of the church, it rose to this responsibility. Its declarations on the race issue provide a platform of prophetic utterance on which religious leadership can
confidently stand to challenge the indifference and timidity of
the state and of secular bodies. In its deliverance on " The
Social Bases of a Just and Durable Peace," Delaware defined
in unmistakable fashion the Christian theological basis for
belief in the equality of races, it outlined the relation of the
race issue to world peace and peace within the American nation, it acknowledged the sins of the past, and it frankly faced
the implications of its position within the affairs of the
churches themselves. So far-reaching, so bold a series of utterances deserves attention in some detail.

To begin with, Delaware laid down the fundamental theological belief on which the Christian faith rests and in the light of which racial discrimination appears as something abhorrent in the eyes of God:

Man is a child of God and all men are brothers one of another. The church in its long-established missionary work recognizes its responsibility to bring all men into full relationship as children of God.

Mankind is one in nature and in the sight of God. No group of men is inherently superior or inferior to any other, and none is above any other beloved of God.

James Russell Lowell once spoke of the New Testament as "dynamite." Christianity has often been characterized as "revolutionary." If Christianity at any period appears to lack revolutionary power, if the dynamite fails to explode, the explanation lies in the failure of the church to believe the basic principles of its own gospel, such as have been expressed again in the foregoing paragraphs from the Delaware declaration. Generations of Christian history and struggle lie behind every sentence. The whole Christian missionary enterprise is here in doctrinal embryo, and on no other basis can it go forward. Here is a religious motivation for struggle against racial superstition and discrimination which cannot, once its truth is accepted, be denied.

From that necessary foundation of Christian teaching, the Delaware Conference moved ahead to declare the necessity for racial justice as a condition of peace:

Among the primary factors in the maintenance of a just and durable peace will be equitable treatment of all racial groups that make up the world's population. Therefore the securing of justice now for racial groups is essential if America is to make its full contribution in securing a just and durable peace.

And in a longer statement the conference placed the responsibility for the racial issue on "the belief that culture is a

product of biological heredity and that Anglo-European culture is superior because it has sprung from superior human
strains." Preservation of full cultural freedom for all peoples
was demanded, and greater cultural interchange. "Assimilation of culture does not mean amalgamation of racial stocks,"
but it does mean a leveling of many present walls of separation.

It cannot be denied that, in the effort to promote racial justice, the United States is likely to prove one of the most recal-
citrant nations. Delaware's delegates faced the realities honestly and with Christian contrition:

We acknowledge with profound contrition the sin of racial
discrimination in American life and our own share, though we are
Christians, in the common guilt. So long as our attitudes and policies deny peoples of other races in our own or other lands the
essential position of brothers in the common family of mankind
we cannot safely be trusted with the making of a just and durable
peace.

That last sentence probably should be printed in italics.
Print it in italics in your own mind by reading it aloud to
yourself. This passage in the Delaware report continues:

In our own country millions of people, especially American
Negroes, are subjected to discrimination and unequal treatment in
educational opportunities, in employment, wages and conditions
of work, in access to professional and business opportunities, in
housing, in transportation, in the administration of justice and
even in the right to vote. We condemn all such inequalities and
call upon our fellow Christians and fellow citizens to initiate
and support measures to establish equality of status and treatment
of members of minority racial and cultural groups.

And then, to drive the same point home, the conference came
back to another declaration concerning "the crucial importance of justice in race relations in our own country as paving
the way for the wider recognition of it which will be essential

to world peace." It acknowledged that the rebuff dealt the Oriental demand for a recognition of the principle of race equality at the Paris Peace Conference, and the adoption of racial discrimination as a principle of American immigration policy, had played a part in bringing on another World War. It pledged, in the face of popular feeling which at the very time the Delaware Conference was in session was sweeping more than seventy thousand American citizens of Japanese descent into concentration camps, to protect the civil rights of these citizens.[8]

Alert to give credit where it was deserved, Delaware praised President Roosevelt for his efforts to lessen discriminations against Negroes in public services and war industries. But it asked that, " when further statements of peace aims are made," the United States " clarify in more detail its peace aims toward recognizing racial equality, opportunity and aid for migration, and protection of religious, political, racial and cultural minorities."

These delegates from the Christian churches might have been content to leave the issue there, calling upon government to make clear its program for dealing with the race problem. But a saving sense of prophetic responsibility to their own institution would not permit them to do so. They could not be content to tell the state, or American society, what was required in the way of racial justice if future peace was to be made

[8] In this connection, it should be said that since the Delaware Conference the church forces of America have taken the lead in demanding better treatment for the Japanese-Americans and Japanese interned in what have been euphemistically called " relocation centers." The churches have not only carried on an intelligent and incessant agitation against the worst abuses of the system for dealing with these war victims first inaugurated by the government but have provided a solid core of resistance to the effort to whip up mass hysteria promoted by organizations like the American Legion, the Native Sons of California, certain Pacific coast commercial bodies and political demagogues like Congressman Martin Dies and the majority of his notorious congressional committee.

secure. They felt under compulsion to face the ugly fact of racial discrimination within the Christian institution itself. "Let judgment begin in the house of God!" So they wrote, in words which have not yet begun to pass current among the American churches but which, when they do, will produce powerful effects:

We call our fellow Christians to witness that it is in the nature of the church that Negro men and women and those belonging to other racial and national minorities should be welcomed into the membership, administrative personnel and fellowship of our churches, local and national. We urge individual Christians and the corporate body of the Church of Christ to take up the cross of courageous service in action which deals with the problems of race and color in our land.

It may be said that one measure of the sincerity with which the church presses for racial justice as between nations and on a world scale will be furnished by the demonstration which it gives of its readiness, or lack of readiness, to apply the admonitions of the foregoing paragraph to its own life.

These Delaware declarations on race can hardly be regarded as a definitive program for dealing with the issue on an international basis and in its domestic manifestations. There are gaps; sudden silences; here and there the whisper of prudence is to be heard from the background supplied by American society. But the American church did strike notes of authentic prophetic authority in these deliverances; it did not cry "Peace, peace," where there is no peace; it did not try to escape from its obligation as critic of society and of the state. In view of the later distressing silence of those who formulated the Six Pillars, and of the Princeton Conference, this loyalty at Delaware to the requirements of a Christian order is the more notable. In future days when the race issue, if ignored or evaded, may grow into mankind's greatest torment, this dis-

charge of the prophetic function at Delaware may be accounted
to the church for righteousness.

VII

I believe that it is more difficult to discuss the race question
on a basis of scientific inquiry, moral analysis, the requirements
of statesmanship — or indeed on any basis other than ingrained
prejudice and vocal passion — than any other major issue now
confronting mankind. That is one indication of its importance
and enormous danger. When a question becomes too hot for
calm discussion, then look out for trouble.

I trust that nothing said in this chapter will give rise to a
belief that I regard this as a simple problem. On the contrary,
I know that it is an infinitely involved and difficult problem,
and that with the best will and most determined purpose no
swift solution will be found. When I hear it said that discussion of the racial issue should be left to those who have to live
with it more intimately and continuously than do I, there are
times when I find myself in considerable sympathy with that
point of view. After all, the white who lives in a Mississippi
county in the heart of the "black belt" may be forgiven a
certain amount of impatience with the man who appears to
pontificate on the color question from a northern suburb which
employs unofficial real estate restrictions to exclude all but
whites.

Nevertheless, I cannot conclude this chapter without drawing attention to one more element in the world situation which
bears directly on the racial crisis. That element is the existence of Soviet Russia — a vast land, now spreading like the
heavens above Asia and Europe, making its presence felt wherever the dispossessed and exploited of earth meet to discuss
their lot and their future. It is one of the fundamental social
doctrines of that land that there shall be no racial discrimination within the U.S.S.R. And this is not simply a doctrine; it

is a fact of Russian life. Racial bars have been leveled within Soviet Russia. No man's opportunity is conditioned by the color of his skin. Hence we see the great American singer and actor, Paul Robeson, taking his family to Moscow so that his son can attend schools in a country which knows no color bar.

Here is a fact with which the rest of the white world must increasingly reckon. The state must reckon with it. Soon it will become one of the most potent influences in international affairs. When Asia — soon to be followed by Africa — comes into the gathering place of nations to demand recognition of racial equality, that demand will present no problem to the representatives of Russia. There will be no such pitiful hesitation and dodging on their part as we have seen characterized men like President Wilson, Colonel House, Lord Robert Cecil and General Smuts at Paris in 1919. On the contrary, the representatives of Soviet Russia will hail the raising of that issue. They will say to the delegates from non-white lands: "Of course there must be racial equality! That is what we have always believed; that is what we practice!" That instant agreement will register in international circles.

Capitalist society must reckon with this fact. Today the colored races are the dispossessed, the exploited. The social stigma attaching to their color has become the outward and visible sign of their dispossession and exploitation. If they see a social order in actual operation which knows no such color stigma, what is to be expected but that they will conclude that such an order offers also an end of exploitation? Communist society need not preach its doctrines to rivet the attention and gain the confidence of the colored world. It has only to continue to demonstrate its freedom from color prejudice.

And the Christian church must reckon with this fact. This Russia is officially atheist. It denies there is a God. It calls religion an opiate. But it practices racial equality. In so far as this race issue is concerned, it comes closer to practicing brotherhood than any other nation containing mixed racial stocks. Already we have noted that racial discrimination reaches its most aggravated legal forms in countries which call themselves Christian and which are dominantly Protestant in their cultural backgrounds. If the Christian church is content to go on preaching one thing and seeing its membership, its own agencies and the society of 'Christian' nations practice another, what will be the natural and indeed inevitable inference reached by the colored peoples?

Russia — atheist Russia, communist Russia — with its race equality is more than a revolutionary phenomenon. It is a major force at work in the world; a force which is pushing us all — churches and governments and social orders — before a new bar of historic judgment.

CHAPTER VII

WHO SHALL BE ARMED?

I

Postwar problems are of two sorts — the immediate and the long-range. One immediate problem with long-range consequences is that of disarmament. What nations in the postwar world are to be armed? What nations are to be disarmed? And how is the process of disarmament to be carried out?

During the years of the Long Armistice many minds became oppressed with a fear of the munitions industry as a contributing cause of war. At one period, shortly after the appearance of the book, *Merchants of Death*, and the conclusion of the Nye investigation, there was a tendency in some quarters to place major responsibility for the outbreak of the first World War on armament races and the competition of firms engaged in the international arms trade. The disarmament conferences which met at frequent intervals until after Hitler had rearmed Germany were hailed by all humane-minded persons as steps toward enduring peace. Their main shortcoming seemed to be, however, that with the exception of the Washington Conference most of them adjourned after evolving formulas for disarmament which actually permitted, or even required, the expansion of existing fleets. Russian spokesmen during that period took a sardonic satisfaction in declaring that the Soviet Union was at any time ready to engage in general and complete disarmament, but would accept no substitutes.

At the moment, popular opinion has swung to the other extreme. It is now widely believed that disarmament was a fatal will-o'-the-wisp which the nations pursued only to place themselves at the mercy of the fascist states. Mr. Lippmann now writes of the " exorbitant folly of the Washington Disarmament Conference," and declares that peace is dependent — and has been for a hundred years — on British-American sea power. The theories of Admiral Mahan, held in low repute throughout the 1920's, have again come into their own. Secretary Knox vows that never again will American warships be sunk in a disarmament conference. And the man in the street seems to accept as axiomatic the proposition that world peace requires the concentration of overwhelming military power in the hands of nations which can be trusted with its use — which is to say, of course, in our hands and in the hands of our allies.

Nevertheless, there are still those who are uneasy. They are none too sure that we can be trusted to use vast military power with wisdom, and they are still less sure that dependence can be placed in those who are today our allies. "Power," said Lord Acton in another phrase which has been worn threadbare but still has its bearing on this problem, " power always corrupts; and absolute power corrupts absolutely." It is not easy to stand up against the prevailing winds of opinion at a time when one's own nation is planning to maintain a fleet large enough to control the seven seas and a permanent army of at least two and a half million men. But there are those who are still unconvinced that arming one group of nations and disarming another group means permanent peace, or that general disarmament is a policy calculated to encourage international brigandage.

So we are going into the postwar period with divided minds.

II

The common man — if for the purpose of this discussion we may assume for the moment that any common man exists — seemingly has a very simple and sharply defined picture as to what should be done about armaments after the war. There must be, he argues, an overwhelming victory over the Axis, culminating in the unconditional surrender of the Axis nations. It will be well if, in the course of achieving that victory, the principal Axis nations can be thoroughly laid waste, so that their people shall be made thoroughly familiar with all the horrors of war. What the common man in America or England wants, in other words, is that his opposite number in Germany or Japan shall be personally and unforgettably hammered; let him " get a bellyful of it," so that he will want no more war forever.

Once the Axis nations have been thus chastened, the common man wants to see them completely disarmed. He is even inclined at times to protest against leaving them so much as domestic police forces; if policing is to be done, let the victorious nations do it. But if this seems unnecessarily Draconian, and at odds with the general desire to " get the boys home again " at the earliest possible moment, then let care be taken that police forces are that and nothing else, and that their numbers do not exceed the minimum required to maintain domestic order.

Once the Axis nations have been thus completely disarmed, let them be kept that way. Let their factories be put under incessant supervision, so that no new war material can be surreptitiously manufactured. Let their officer castes be forced into civilian employment. Let their war offices be abolished. At frequent intervals, let there be inspections made by the concert of United Nations, and if any evidence of secret rearmament is uncovered, let there be swift and drastic punishment.

Do all this, and there will be no more trouble.

Now this picture in the common man's mind, it must be recognized, corresponds very closely with the program announced by President Roosevelt and Prime Minister Churchill in the Atlantic Charter. The eighth provision in that document reads:

They [the United Nations] believe that all the nations of the world, for realistic as well as spiritual reasons, must come to the abandonment of the use of force. Since no future peace can be maintained if land, sea or air armaments continue to be employed by nations which threaten, or may threaten, aggression outside of their frontiers, they believe, pending the establishment of a wider and permanent system of general security, that the disarmament of such nations is essential. They will likewise aid and encourage all other practicable measures which will lighten for peace-loving peoples the crushing burden of armaments.

There are some fine phrases in this declaration. Abandonment of force by all nations is stated as the ultimate ideal. Practicable (*sic!*) measures which will lighten the burden of armaments on the people of the peace-loving nations — which means us and our allies — are promised encouragement. But the nub of Point 8 is the announcement that nations which " threaten, or may threaten, aggression outside their frontiers " — which means our present enemies — are to be immediately and fully disarmed.

In other words, the Atlantic Charter takes the same position as was taken on this issue by the Peace of Versailles. That treaty, in introducing the section dealing with disarmament, resorted to reassuring words concerning a policy of general demilitarization to be carried out at some later, unspecified date: " In order to render possible the initiation of general limitation of the armaments of all nations, Germany undertakes strictly to observe the military, naval and air clauses which follow." But those clauses which followed provided for the unilateral and immediate disarmament of Germany. They went into effect; the vague promise of " general limitation of the armaments of all nations " never became more than a pious hope.

But does this program for the disarmament of the Axis, as laid down by the American and British leaders and concurred in by the masses in their countries, have universal support throughout the United Nations? As these words are written, it begins to appear that it does not. And this opposition to unilateral disarmament is not the negligible opposition of pacifists or of groups without political influence; it comes from a quarter which is controlled by Stalin and may be presumed to voice his views.

The "National Committee of Free Germany" (*Freies Deutschland*), organized in Russia among German war prisoners, has drawn up a manifesto calling on Germans to rise against the Hitlerite regime. This manifesto has been scattered over Germany in millions of copies tossed from Russian planes. It clearly promises that any such German government formed by revolt against Hitler will be armed, and that such elements in the army as take part in the revolt will be continued in the armed forces of the new German state. It is, of course, impossible that any such committee could have been formed in Russia, any such manifesto written, or any such promises scattered broadcast over the German lines without the approval of the Russian authorities, which means Stalin.

Evidently there is here a deviation between Anglo-American and Russian policy which requires clearing up.

III

There are, however, certain questions about a policy of one-sided disarmament which need to be considered, whatever the positions of the leading United Nations. I suggest that we ask ourselves at least three.

First, will a policy of unilateral (the diplomatic word for one-sided) disarmament work? The common man will answer that of course it will work. If I have all the guns, and you haven't any guns, you won't attack me, will you? Then

why suggest that there can be any argument over the answer
to such a question?

But that is to ignore history. Recent history, at that. Remember what happened after the first World War. Germany
was disarmed. Not *totally* disarmed, to be sure, but disarmed
to such an extent that her army was reduced to the size of the
army of one of the lesser Balkan powers. Her heavy artillery
was entirely taken away from her. Her navy was sunk. Her
air force was wiped out. She was forbidden to continue con-
scription. Provision was made for inspection to see that she
did not secretly rearm. All that was left of her former military might was a volunteer army of 100,000 men — hardly
more than a police force in a nation of seventy millions. Then,
as if to make the process of disarmament sure, her finances col-
lapsed and her government went broke.

Yet Germany rearmed. She rearmed so rapidly and on such
a scale that, twenty years after Versailles, she was again ready
to challenge the world, and did so with forces which, between
the invasion of Poland and the fall of France, won the most
spectacular succession of victories in European history. What
had happened? The story is too long to tell here, and some of
it is still shrouded in secrecy. But we know that, in the main,
it was a story of intrigue within the ranks of the victorious
nations.

Germany had been disarmed to preserve the status quo established at Versailles. But there were nations, some of them on
the winning side in the first World War, which were not satisfied with the division of spoils or with other provisions of that
treaty. Italy began to intrigue against the treaty before it had
been signed. A whole group of " revisionist " states grew up
in Europe. Russia needed technical help in the forging of her
new armies; she was glad to offer Germany's officers opportunity to continue their studies behind the protection of the
Russian frontier. England became afraid of French policy;

she found means of encouraging German resurgence, finally, and without consulting her old ally, to the extent of authorizing Germany to rebuild her navy. All the world turned in to set the Reich back on its financial feet.[1]

It is this element of susceptibility to intrigue which wrecks a program of unilateral disarmament. Suppose Germany were again disarmed after this war, while the great European victors remained armed to the hilt. How long would it be before astute Germans would begin to plant the idea in British minds that, unless some sort of rampart were thrown across western Europe, communism would sweep to the English Channel — and then what would happen to the stocks and bonds of the London " City," or to the lands and coronets and precedence of the ruling classes? Or how long would it be before they would begin to point out that the checks administered to British policy on the Continent would not continue once there was a strong power on the Rhine to support London against the pretensions of Moscow? And if this did not work — or work to a sufficient degree — how long would it be before other astute Germans would be planting the idea in Russian minds that a capitalist Britain was not to be trusted, but that a foresighted Soviet Union would see the advantage of having a strongly armed friendly power in the path of any attack from the west?

That is the sort of intrigue which any disarmed nation will seek to carry on between armed neighbors. Do you say it would not work this time — that Russia and Britain would be on their guard and that their understanding is so complete as

[1] The nineteenth chapter of Clemenceau's book, *Grandeur and Misery of Victory*, is devoted to showing how easily a unilaterally disarmed nation, by taking advantage of the divergencies between the interests of the armed, can rearm in such a way as to elude the policing powers of the victors, even though they may know all — or almost all — about what is going on. This chapter is also valuable for its disclosure of the part which Russia played in the German rearmament.

to be proof against such undermining? Perhaps it would not work in one year after the war's close. But in five? In ten? In twenty? Remember again what happened between 1919 and 1939.

The second question which I suggest for consideration is this: In the event of unilateral disarmament, will the private munitions industry be satisfied to leave the disarmed nations disarmed?

There is serious reason to doubt it. The callous disregard for consequences shown by munitions manufacturers in the past constitutes one of the most disgraceful pages in the history of capitalistic enterprise. Not even the distiller has shown as little compunction with regard to the social results of his business. The standard technique of the " merchant of death " has been to build up the forces of one nation against another by manufacturing war threats, corrupting cabinets and parliaments, and creating a vicious circle in which fears have been played off against fears until a tension had been created which had to snap somewhere. The records compiled by the Senate investigation in this country and by the parliamentary inquiry in England (even though that was seriously hamstrung by the munitions firms, all of which had high official connections) showed that no treaty, no agreement, no legal restrictions of any kind were sufficient to daunt most munitions salesmen when once their sensitive nostrils had caught the whiff of a fat contract.

A disarmed nation is a standing invitation to the avarice of the private munitions firm. It will use all its connections — and these are always powerful — to assist the sort of intrigue we have already mentioned as a preliminary to rearmament. And once it has succeeded in creating suspicion between the armed nations, so that the way has been opened to do business with the previously disarmed, it will sell — for a profit — any secrets it may possess concerning the armaments of other nations, in order to increase the size of its orders. While the international armament ring continues to operate as private, competitive business — and there has yet to be heard any official proposal to deprive it of its profit-seeking status after the war — I do not believe that it is within the possibilities of its nature to be content while a disarmed nation remains disarmed.

The third question is one which should occur immediately to any person of thoughtful mind. If the Axis nations are disarmed at the end of this war, what need is there for the United Nations to remain armed? Why should nations which will be struggling under war debts of unprecedented size be required to go on adding to those debts in order to sustain the enormous military establishments which are apparently contemplated? Is not this the logical time, the safest time, to put the whole world on a disarmed basis?

IV

All this the representatives of the churches who met at Delaware seem to have seen. At any rate, after naming " limitation of armaments " as one of the " preconditions of a just and durable peace " which " require changes of national policy on the part of the United States," the conference adopted this as its eighth Guiding Principle:

We believe that military establishments should be internationally controlled and be made subject to law under the community of nations. For one or more nations to be forcibly deprived of their arms while other nations retain the right of maintaining or expanding their military establishments can only produce an uneasy peace for a limited period. Any initial arrangement which falls short of this must therefore be looked upon as temporary and provisional.

Here was plain, decisive speech. Whether it was too plain I have no means of knowing, but it is a lamentable fact that by the time the Six Pillars of Peace were formulated the voice of the church on this issue had sunk to this faint whisper:

The peace must establish procedures for controlling military establishments everywhere.

Only that and nothing more! Not a word in it that any government — including Hitler's — might not have subscribed to, and then proceeded to interpret as it pleased! Fortunately, the Princeton Conference was later partially to retrieve the ground which the Six Pillars threw away. But only partially. For even Princeton said nothing to suggest to the nations that disarmament, to be a dependable agent of lasting peace, must be multilateral.

This was the Princeton declaration:

That drastic reduction in armaments be undertaken as steps toward the goals envisaged in the Atlantic Charter of the "abandonment of the use of force" and lifting from the peoples of the world "the crushing burden of armaments."

Here was at least recognition that it was "drastic reduction in armaments" which was being sought; that was better than vague words about "procedures for controlling military establishments." However, one cannot help wondering whether knowledge that the American and British governments had committed themselves, in the Atlantic Charter, to one-sided disarmament, made the Princeton delegates speak cautiously at this point. Certainly the direct reference to the Atlantic Charter suggests that they were fully conscious of the disarmament policies of that document. One suspects, therefore, that the Princeton deliverance, in respect of this issue, represented an effort by church delegates to speak right up to the limits set by the declarations of their governments, but not to step beyond those limits.

At any rate, there could be no clearer demonstration of the

weakness, the irrelevance, the wishy-washyness which comes
upon the church when, in dealing with public issues, it deserts
for a moment its prophetic calling and is content to echo the
voice of political expediency. Delaware fell into no such trap.
Its words were not to be dismissed with a yawn. It knew the
workings of the moral order, and so it looked the authors of
the Atlantic Charter in the eye and said: "For one or more nations to be forcibly deprived of their arms while other nations
retain the right of maintaining or expanding their military establishments can only produce an uneasy peace for a limited
period." In other words, if the United Nations attempt the
unilateral disarmament of their enemies, let them know that
they will thus gain only a short respite in which to carry out
their own disarmament. And if, in the period of that respite,
they fail themselves to disarm, then let them know that they
will again have condemned their peoples to slaughter.

At once timorous souls begin to twitter about 'policing.'
Won't international brigands infest the highways of the world
if we all disarm? Must there not be force available to preserve
international law and order, and to exact obedience to the dic-
tates of the eventual world government? We have already
considered this matter of policing, and do not need to discuss
it again at length.[2] But this may be reiterated: The problem
of international policing will be a comparatively simple one in
a disarmed world. Only in a world where some of the nations
are armed and some disarmed will policing become a task to
require great forces and such statesmanship as nations seldom
produce.

The church, then, must speak for general, immediate postwar disarmament. It must appeal to the operations of the moral
order and to the lessons of history to instruct the nations that
this, and this alone, will make for enduring peace. It will
be laughed at as visionary; it will be attacked as subversive of

[2] See pages 55–58.

world order. But it must persist, for to demand anything less is to be recreant to its own best insights.

And is the church indeed guilty of a lack of realism in thus insisting on general, immediate disarmament? Secular leaders are notoriously timid about taking anything but the traditional "strong line" in this field. They fear that to support national policies of disarmament will expose them to the charge of lack of patriotism. But here is a national leader who has had an international experience, in the last war, in the intrigues which accompanied and followed Versailles and in the diplomacy of the Long Armistice period, which gives his words unusual importance. He is generally regarded as a man of conservative nature; certainly his political following has been largely composed of those who take pride in "keeping their feet on the ground." I am referring, of course, to the former President of the United States, Herbert Hoover, and on the question of realism in relation to armaments I wish to quote certain passages from the book which he, in company with former Ambassador Hugh Gibson, has written.

Listen, for if there is any such thing as the "Voice of Experience" with relation to this particular matter, this is it speaking:

Disarmament offers the only effective way to bring militarism under control. . . . The Treaty of Versailles contained a pious pledge of all the Allies to disarm sometime, but made no provision for when or how. The opposition among the victorious nations was rooted partly in fears that security could be provided only with overwhelming armies and navies. It came in part from mutual distrust among the former Allies themselves. Military alliances sprang up at once. The essence of military alliance is large armed force, and alliances are at once a block to disarmament. The heightened nationalism which arose inevitably from the war also contributed to each country's desire for arms. Arms were made easily accessible to the liberated nations by extensive sales from the larger Allies on credit. And there was the grim fact that masses of professional soldiers had been created who wanted to hold their jobs. To some extent, war industries wished to continue their markets. . . .

Human nature and human mores being what they are, all this will happen again unless positive measures are taken immediately while the world is sick of killing and wants action to end it. The opportunity for comprehensive action will be of short duration. Unless this opportunity is seized upon, all these same obstructions will grow again — nationalism, imperialism, military alliances — and the witches fear, hate and revenge will mix a new brew. They all demand armies and oppose disarmament.

Therefore, experience shows if there is to be a reduction of arms among the victorious nations, it must be agreed upon in advance and action should take place within weeks, not months or years, after the firing ceases.[8]

Mr. Hoover of course holds that the war must be followed by the disarmament of the Axis nations, as I could show by more extended quotation. But the point of greatest importance is that, speaking from experience such as few living men can parallel, he warns that if there is not to be a recrudescence of all the evils of nationalism and imperialism in the postwar world, there must be immediate disarmament after the end of the fighting of the United Nations also. " Action should take place within weeks, not months or years, after the firing ceases." In other words, this sober, conservative but greatly experienced secular leader offers testimony in this fashion that the prophetic demand of the church for immediate, general postwar disarmament is the essence of realism.

v

Of all the shifting sands on which to try to build a stable structure of peace and world order, surely the most insecure

---

[8] From *The Problems of Lasting Peace*, by Herbert Hoover and Hugh Gibson. New York: Doubleday, Doran & Company, Inc., 1942. Quoted by permission. The italics are Mr. Hoover's.

is the idea that the world is divided between righteous and un-righteous nations, and that wisdom and justice require that the righteous shall restrain the unrighteous.

However, there is another delusion which, if accepted, will almost as quickly and just as surely undermine any international order. That is the delusion that the interests of nations allied in war remain identical in peace. They do not. And the result is that nations which end a war armed *with* each other presently find themselves armed *against* each other.

Since these things are true — and all our experience proves that they are true — there is neither moral ground nor political wisdom to justify a policy of one-sided postwar disarmament. If the victorious nations persist in it, the very stars in their courses will operate to prove its folly. The Christian church, when it calls for complete disarmament, is calling for the only action of the nations which will preserve an order of peace. Then why should it ever consent to speak in mere echo of the voices of nations which are headed for disaster? Here, if anywhere, the church has a moral responsibility to discharge. It has no business echoing the state. Its business, its responsibility, is to challenge the state. For world peace — disarmament, complete and immediate!

CHAPTER VIII

On the Treatment of Enemies

I

In June 1943 *Fortune* polled what it believed to be a representative cross section of the American people with this question: " What should we do with Germany if we win the war? " The answers were tabulated thus:

Set up a United Nations council to rule Germany for ten years or so and eventually make her accept a democratic government and see that she sticks to it	36.9%
Bring to trial and execute all found to be leading Nazi officials	31.5
Make Germany use all her available men, money and materials to rebuild the damage done in other countries	27.2
Set up an international government and rule Germany for 100 years	20.7
Do nothing to Germany but see to it that she stays within her own borders	13.2
Carve Germany up and divide her among some of the United Nations	11.2
Kill a Nazi for every person killed by the Germans in occupied countries	3.7
No reply or don't know	6.9

I quote this poll not because of the light which it casts on the American mind as it contemplates an issue it must face on the day Hitler surrenders, but because it casts so little light. There is so little approach to unanimity, so much confusion of thought that, if the poll reveals anything, it is that the American people have yet to make up their minds about what to do with their enemies.

Yet one can sense an undertone of anger, a general — although still unformulated — expectation that something shall be done to Germany sufficiently severe to punish her according to the extent of the suffering which she is held responsible for having brought upon mankind. If the poll had asked the same question concerning Japan, the answers would probably have reflected even more unmistakably this demand for drastic punishment.

This war has not witnessed, at least in Britain and the United States, any such excesses of personal vindictiveness, or any such organized campaigns to whip up mass hatred, as darkened the last conflict. In the United States the effort of the chairman of the War Writers' Board, Rex Stout, to preach the duty of hatred as a means of winning the war met with instant rebuke from all parts of the country. In Great Britain the proposal to introduce hate-inflaming exercises in the training of British soldiers was vigorously condemned by the general commanding the forces in the British Isles. In neither country has there been any particular feeling against the Italians.

American opinion has been bitter against the Japanese, and there have been sporadic efforts to foment this feeling. But it has been a bitterness touched with chagrin, a resentment caused by charges of foul play and by a suspicion that the Japanese outsmarted us. No American likes to be outsmarted. Victory, when it comes, will do much to assuage what is in reality a species of wounded vanity.

Nevertheless, there are evidences of mounting pressure for drastic treatment of enemies in the hour of victory. The governments-in-exile have been insistent that Germany shall pay to the limit for the brutalities of which her troops have been guilty in occupied countries. Both Mr. Roosevelt and Mr. Eden have given official assurances that there will be exemplary punishment of the Germans responsible for all such atrocities. Russia has never ceased, while making a distinction between the German people and what she calls the "Nazi fascists," to promise dire retribution for the Nazi leaders. She has tried to make sure that Anglo-American support for that policy would prove more than verbal by pressing for immediate trial and punishment for Rudolf Hess. And throughout the British public, subjected to the terror of the air blitz and the long strain of the war, there is a rising demand for vengeance, according to the English observer, Stephen Spender.

When he returned from a visit to England in the summer of 1942 Dr. Walter W. Van Kirk, one of the secretaries of the Federal Council of Churches, warned that "there are indications that the poison of an uncontrollable vindictiveness is eating its way into the minds and hearts of vast numbers of people in the conquered lands of Europe. While in England I was told that the names and addresses of thousands of Quislings and of Nazi functionaries in the Lowlands are being secretly filed in anticipation of what is described as 'Axing Day.' I was informed that all the axes and hatchets in Holland have been bought up and laid away against the day of the Great Revenge."[1] A terrible fate seems in store for the Germans scattered among the nations conquered by Hitler. That probably includes the Germans in Italy, provided any are left there after the German armies have retreated from that peninsula.

The Christian church cannot avoid speaking on this problem, for it is one on which thoughtful men everywhere are seeking moral guidance. It cannot be indifferent to the responsibility which rests upon the Nazis, the Italian Fascists and the Japanese militarists for hastening the return to world warfare. It does not ascribe sole guilt to them; it acknowledges the responsibility which all the nations must share for destruction of the

[1] From an article, "British Churches in the Crisis," in the *Christian Century* for September 9, 1942. Quoted by permission.

hope of peace. Yet it does believe that the fascist mind and spirit has deliberately and unceasingly pushed the world toward war. What shall be done to the fascist states? The Christian church knows that hosts of men are asking of it that question. It also knows that it must, as the Christian church, live for the long years to come with the answer which it gives.

II

In general, it seems to me that three schools of thought concerning the treatment of Germany can be distinguished. (It will be simpler to keep this discussion in terms of the treatment of Germany. Such slight differences as apply in the case of Japan can be indicated later.) The first group is well typified by Lord Vansittart, who leads a " Never Again Movement," as it has been called, in England. Lord Vansittart was for many years, as Sir Robert Vansittart, the permanent undersecretary of the Foreign Office. That is to say, he was the top man in the Foreign Office aside from the Foreign Minister himself. And while Foreign Ministers came and went with the tides of politics, Sir Robert stayed on, year after year instructing those Foreign Ministers in the continuing and permanent lines of Britain's foreign policy. Needless to say, there are few more influential figures among England's 'ruling classes.' That term has been no misnomer when applied to Sir Robert. For years, he really ruled.

Lord Vansittart's " Never Again Movement " rests on one premise — that the Germans are inherently, biologically brutal, ruthless and given to making war, and that in order to keep them from destroying the peace of Europe in the future they must, when defeated, be subjected to the severest repression which can be contrived. " The German," says the jacket of Vansittart's pamphlet, *Black Record*, " has always been the barbarian, the war power, the enemy — furtive or avowed — of humanitarianism, liberalism and Christian civilization, and the

Hitler regime is no accidental phenomenon but the logical fruit of German history, the German *in excelsis*." On that basis, of course, the only logical thing to do with Germany is to pulverize her. This time there must be a peace treaty free from the sentimental weakness of Versailles.

How much following Lord Vansittart has in England it would be hard to say; probably a good deal more than the liberal press or the church forces would like to admit. That he has followers — unconscious followers, in all likelihood — in the United States, there can be no doubt. Thus the columnist, Westbrook Pegler, has told the millions of newspaper readers who follow his views that the only true war aim of the United Nations is " the extermination of the German nation as a menace to the peace and safety of the world. . . . Their lands should be taken over by outright conquest and de-Germanized, though it takes a hundred years to exterminate the spirit that makes them so dangerous. . . . It will be a messy task . . . but the Allied armies are now teaching their soldiers that they must be tough and kill, and the various governments of the victorious countries when this war is done should be just as tough in their execution of their phase of the task."

Nor is this feeling confined to the slapdash of daily journalism. The chairman of the department of history at the University of Chicago (what does that title call up in your mind? Coolness, impartiality, the careful weighing of evidence — qualities like that?) insists that the treatment of Germany after surrender shall be as punitive as it can be made. And then the chairman of the department of history at the University of Chicago (the place where President Robert Maynard Hutchins is showing the rest of the American colleges how a college should be conducted) proceeds to explain that " the program here set forth is based on the conviction that the Germans are not like Frenchmen or Britishers or Americans but possess certain national traits which make them impervious to reason, generosity or even fair play." Note the way in which Professor Bernadotte E. Schmitt sweeps all Germans into one company of the damned. It is not *some* Germans, or even *many* Germans; it is *the* Germans — all of them — who are "impervious to reason, generosity or even fair play." Naturally, on this basis Germany is to be flung beneath the iron plowshare of implacable retribution; her towns and fields are to be sown with salt.

This, then, is the first school of thought: Germany is a nation of wild beasts, to be dealt with as one would deal with ravaging beasts. Recently this idea has been slightly modified in certain quarters, to the extent of holding that Germany is a nation of dangerous paranoids, to be dealt with as insane. Psychiatrists of standing have given their professional endorsement to this diagnosis. One wonders if these men who say with such confidence, " The Germans are this " or " The Germans are that," and then proceed to propose appropriate punishments, have ever heard of Edmund Burke: " You cannot draw up an indictment against a whole people."

A second, and much more important, school of thought finds its best expression in Dr. William Temple, the Archbishop of Canterbury. While still Archbishop of York, Dr. Temple worked out the series of recommendations for the postwar treatment of Germany which first appeared in magazine form and, I understand, are now to be found in his book, *The Hope of a New World*. Because of the influence of his position and the rigorous quality of his mind, the argument by which the Archbishop arrives at his conclusion deserves careful attention.

The Christian ethic, the Archbishop agrees, teaches forgiveness of enemies. But forgiveness, according to the pattern set by Christ on the cross, is impossible in this case, for that pattern requires self-immolation, and no nation is prepared for that. Therefore the infliction of a just penalty for wrongdoing is nearer to a Christian solution of the problem of treatment of a defeated enemy than any other which is practically achievable, since this will at least not condone wrong. Germany, accordingly, must be punished for her wrongdoing; three times within three-quarters of a century she has devastated Europe by carefully planned aggression.

What form should this punishment take? The Archbishop proposes that the period of the coming peace be divided into two parts, the first a period of " interim settlement " covering " perhaps five years," and the second, and following, the period of " permanent settlement." The period of the interim settlement " should be in part penal." " One suggestion which deserves careful consideration is that the ancient German nations should be reconstituted as they were before the rise of Bismarck. . . . These states should for a time be garrisoned by the Allies; but it must always be understood that before the final settlement is made they shall be free to come together in any way that they themselves choose to make again a united Germany." This course would be followed as " a necessary preliminary to the re-education of the German mind, vitiated by years of German propaganda." After this preliminary penal period had supposedly punished the Germans sufficiently for their propensity to war, there should then be a permanent peace settlement drawn in an international conference in which the Germans would participate as equal negotiators.

The Archbishop apparently wishes to find a way " to bring home to Germany the moral condemnation which she has earned," while not embittering the German people. He warns that " there must be no new generation growing up under the embittering conditions of a penal peace," and in a statement issued a little more than a year after his original proposal he declared that " we must look forward to renewed fellowship [with the German people], and consequently, while the settlements are bound to be such as would appear severe to the German state, they must also secure to the ordinary German citizen an even chance of sharing the benefits of civilization with his neighbors, providing his state is itself behaving as a good neighbor among them." One wonders, however, how he expects to inflict five years of penalty, with Germany broken into bits and all the economic hardships this would entail, without engendering bitterness among the German people. Penalties of the sort the Archbishop envisages do not fall, in their punitive effect, on a disembodied " state." They fall on the people who are the citizens of that state.[2]

III

This brings us to the third school of thought, which seeks an entirely different kind of postwar treatment for Germany. Because I am persuaded that such policies as are advocated by both the schools previously considered would sow the seeds of future war, as well as work out in actual excesses of retaliation which would eventually revolt the consciences of Britons and Americans, I desire to give extended attention to the thought of this third school. The most satisfactory way in which to do this will be to consider it as presented by its most competent expositor, Edward Hallett Carr.

First a word as to Mr. Carr. Who is he and what does he represent? At the moment, Mr. Carr is that most suspect of beings — a professor. He is, to be specific, the Woodrow Wilson professor of international politics in the University College of Wales. But he has not always been a professor. For years he was a member of the permanent staff of the British Foreign Office — the same staff that produced Lord Vansittart! Then he forsook diplomacy for journalism; he became what the English call a " leader writer " on the London *Times*. In other

[2] All the quotations from the Archbishop (except the last, which was reported in the daily press from London on October 18, 1942) are taken from an article, " International Justice in the New World," which appeared in the *Churchman*, June 1, 1941, and is quoted by permission.

words, he wrote editorials for that most influential of British conservative papers. From the *Times* he went to the class-room. Along the route he had written several books, gaining most attention for one entitled *The Twenty Years' Crisis, 1919–1939*. We have now to do with the most recent of his books, *Conditions of Peace*, and with the chapter in it, " Brit-ain and Germany." Written in England and addressed in the first instance to Englishmen, what Professor Carr has to say needs to be heard around the world.

The Carr thesis opens with a vivid description of the divided state of mind in which we are approaching the issue of dealing with a defeated Germany:

Most British people are thoroughly uneasy, and even shame-faced, in their approach to this problem. They are conscious both of its critical importance and of its extreme complexity. They are painfully aware of the failure of the past twenty years, having the guilty feeling that coercion was applied to Germany at a time when a policy of reconciliation might have succeeded, and recon-ciliation attempted when nothing but coercion could any longer avail. They are desperately afraid of repeating the same mistake.

They know that resentment was a bad counsellor in 1919, yet they find it difficult to resist the conclusion that the reiteration of the same experience within a single generation has justified that resentment. When they listen to those who argue that Germans are and always have been irreclaimably vicious, and that Germany must be treated for an indefinite period after the war as civilized society treats criminals and lunatics, they are embarrassed by an attitude which seems to stand in flagrant contradiction both to Christian and to humanitarian doctrine, and which offers no pros-pect for the future but unending repression and strife. When on the other hand they listen to those who preach reconciliation, they are uncomfortably sensitive to the charge of naïveté and of refusal to learn from experience; and they seek in vain for a convincing solution of an apparently insoluble problem.

In moments of weariness or of righteous indignation, the temptation is strong to believe that the one path to safety lies, not in attempting to win the good will and cooperation of Germany in a future ordering of Europe and the world, but in keeping Germany permanently so weak that we can afford to ignore her inevitable ill will. There is a serious danger that this mood of reckless and short-sighted cynicism may prevail in the immediate postwar period. The sin of certain propagandists is that they seek to perpetuate it by giving it a rational basis.[3]

Dr. Carr rejects the thesis of inherent German wickedness. He takes a sly delight in pointing out that it was a certain Italian journalist, Benito Mussolini by name, who, during the first World War, started the clamor about the Germans today being essentially the same savages whom Tacitus described. Modern German aggression is, of course, admitted, and the influence of the Prussian spirit in producing this is taken into account. But there is a deeper analysis of the economic and historic causes for German aggressiveness in recent decades. It is pointed out, for example, that Germany never fell under the spell of laissez-faire liberalism, so that it is not unnatural that it should be foremost in the ranks of the opponents of such liberalism now that laissez faire is breaking up. And the influence is adduced of the fact that this nation of eighty millions never had its place of paramountcy in Europe as did France in the eighteenth and Britain in the nineteenth century.

Then comes the reminder:

If we remain fully conscious of the darker shades in the German national tradition, it would still be an injustice to assess the place of Germany in modern history without taking equal account of her positive achievements. It is unfair to dwell on the aggressions of Frederick the Great and to ignore the honorable part played by Prussia in the defeat of the aggression of Napoleon. It

[3] From *Conditions of Peace*, by Edward Hallett Carr. New York: The Macmillan Company, 1942. Quoted, as are all the other passages from the same book in this and the next chapter, by permission.

should not be forgotten that the career of Bismarck, often depicted as an unvarying pattern of ruthlessness, contains the Treaty of Prague concluded with Austria after Sadowa in 1866, which ranks with the peace of Vereeniging as one of the wisest peaces of modern times imposed by a victor on a defeated state.

Germans had a chief share in framing the doctrines and the organization of modern socialism; and the modern system of state-controlled social services is almost wholly of German origin. The compulsory insurance of workers against accident, sickness and disablement, as well as old-age pensions, were introduced by Bismarck in Germany before any of them was heard of in any other civilized country. The gradual adoption of similar provisions in Great Britain was largely due to the study and popularization by the early Fabians of German models.

German achievements in art, science and literature may be irrelevant for present purposes. But the striking capacity for large-scale organization developed by Germany in the industrial conditions of the later nineteenth century is a quality whose value and importance in the modern world cannot be gainsaid.

Nothing has occurred to reverse the accepted nineteenth-century judgment on Germans as a patient, thrifty and hard-working people. The modern world is not so richly endowed with ability and resourcefulness that it can light-heartedly cast out from its midst as irredeemably bad a nation possessing, in combination with many grave defects, so many valuable attributes.

It is improbable that the future judgment of history on modern Germany will be painted all in one color, and that color black.

Is postwar Germany to be dealt with on a basis of reprisal and repression? Dr. Carr objects on moral, practical and economic grounds. He believes that, after the war, the conscience of mankind will shrink from a policy which inflicts suffering on individuals who have not been responsible for the wrong-doing of their government. In this connection, he recalls the famous telegram from Lord Plumer, in command of the British occupying troops in Germany after the last war, to the British government. Britain was at that time cooperating with the other Allies to maintain a blockade in order to coerce Germany into signing and observing the Treaty of Versailles. But the sight of German starvation so upset the British soldiers that they insisted on sharing their rations, and the morale of the army of occupation deteriorated to such an extent that the blockade had to be raised to satisfy the soldiers' objections.

Moreover, Dr. Carr insists, there is the factor of youth. The older generation may clamor for a policy of permanent coercion; it has already slipped into a mood of moral pessimism. But not the younger.

After the war the need for reconciliation with an emancipated Germany as the one conceivable way to European peace will gradually assert itself, and will in the end become so strong as to preclude the pursuit of any policy incompatible with it. The younger generation will not be deterred from making the attempt; for in the long run it is better to fail through the excessive faith which attempts the difficult and hazardous task of turning an enemy into a friend than through the excessive cynicism which offers no prospect but the perpetuation of mutual hate. No policy ultimately incompatible with reconciliation can endure, for it will be found morally unbearable. The danger is that it may be pursued long enough to destroy the chance of reconciliation.

On practical grounds, Dr. Carr objects to repression, since political dismemberment could be carried through only at staggering cost, by force and maintained by constant occupation. Economic dismemberment would prove even more difficult and costly. On economic grounds, such a policy would be disastrous, since what Europe so desperately needs is larger, not smaller, economic units.

Then what should be done? Dr. Carr makes five proposals. First, occupy Germany at the close of the war as a means of insuring order. Accompany this occupation with all the humanitarian policies for emergency help that have been suggested. Second, disarm Germany completely. Third, hold the economic penalties laid upon Germany to a minimum, because maximum penalties don't work, and inflict no personal penalties except those which Hitler and his gangsters suffer at the hands of the German people. Fourth, establish a European economic unit in which Germany can attain prosperity. Fifth, give the Germans a sense of their cooperative importance in building a new Europe.

Bear with one more long quotation, for it summarizes the thinking of this British publicist:

We may sum up the main objections to the proposed policy of penalization, dismemberment and permanent coercion of Germany by saying that such a policy would prove in the long run morally repugnant, physically impracticable and economically retrograde. In the first flush of victory it could be imposed by force. But it could not be maintained except by the permanent use of force on a scale which Great Britain and the United States would be unwilling, and no other power or group of powers would be able, to apply; and it would bring economic disaster to Central Europe, which would have damaging repercussions elsewhere.

The discussion leaves us, however, with the necessity of finding a more positive solution. If our conception of a postwar settlement must be based on recognition of Germany's present and future strength, we have to find a way of reconciling this fact with some prospect other than that of either accepting German domination in Europe or fighting a war once a generation to prevent it. There is no guaranteed solution of any political problem, for nothing is proof against human folly and human wickedness. But the elements of the only conceivable solution have already begun to emerge.

The German dilemma can be resolved, not by destroying Germany or by diminishing her, but by making her a partner in a larger unit in which Great Britain will also have her place. Germany's belated nationalism can be overcome only by making internationalism worth her while. Like all lasting political ends, this result can be achieved only by a combination of power and consent. But it is essential that these two processes should be pursued

together, and that coercion should not be so applied as to destroy
the chance of ultimate reconciliation.

IV

I offer no apologies for thus stressing the contribution made
by Professor Carr to the discussion of Germany's postwar
treatment. Every word I have quoted seems to me worth careful weighing, and the total policy presented the essence of political and economic realism. It is my sincere hope that by this
extensive quotation I may induce my readers to go back to the
Carr book, and thus to become familiar with the entire argument. It is with the utmost enthusiasm that I offer this free
advertisement to Dr. Carr's publishers, the Messrs. Macmillan,
trusting that it will add thousands to their circulation of his
book.

But the Carr thesis is particularly important for the purposes
of this study because it so closely parallels the thinking of the
Christian church. At Delaware and again at Princeton the representatives of the church faced this same issue. They recognized its seriousness; they looked forward to the imposition of
some penalty on the states guilty of precipitating war. But
they rejected any policy of reprisal or permanent repression;
they warned against the moral destruction spread by vindictiveness and hate. As means to future peace, they called for inclusion of Germany — and all enemy nations — in works of
constructive cooperation for the rehabilitation of scarred areas
and the development of other regions whose resources are still
unutilized for human welfare.

Concerning this issue of treatment of enemies, New Testament morality is essentially that contained in the admonition of
St. Paul, " Overcome evil with good." But what is good?
Certainly it cannot be revenge or retaliation. Delaware was so
sure on this point that it wrote it into its third Guiding Principle:

We believe that it is contrary to the moral order that nations in their dealings with one another should be motivated by a spirit of revenge and retaliation. Such attitudes will lead, as they always have led, to renewed conflict.

Retaliation is not only a repudiation of the Christian ethic. It is also a policy which fails to work in practice. (Inevitably, for the moral order is arrayed against it.) It was the very sections of the Versailles Treaty which were animated by the spirit of vengeance which broke down most quickly and with most devastating world-wide effect. John Maynard Keynes had warned that they would, basing his argument on economic grounds. The delegates at the peace conference, goaded by public bitterness at home, would not heed. It was the moral order, quite as much as any economic law, which refused to be denied.

"Means must be sought," said Delaware, "effectively to counteract hate and vengeance as controlling motives." "There should be no punitive reparations, no humiliating decrees of war guilt, and no arbitrary dismemberment of nations." Even the proposal to inflict punishment on individual leaders in the enemy nations requires careful examination. It may prove much wiser, much more deterrent for the future, and withal much more in accord with moral law to leave them, as Professor Carr suggests, to the judgment of their own peoples.

There is an illusion about this matter of inflicting punishment on the leaders of enemy countries as it appears to most eyes in time of war. The demand for such punishment during the last war, for example, led to the inclusion in the Treaty of Versailles of Part VII on "Penalties." Article 227 provided for the trial of the Kaiser and Article 228 for the trial of other Germans. The Kaiser was never tried, and the few Germans who were went free. Why? It is the fashion today, while we are again in the midst of war and some of us are again thirsting to find individual evildoers to punish, to say that the trouble was that the Versailles Treaty left the trial of the Kaiser and his aids to German courts and German law, so that when it became apparent that these would not convict, the Allies concluded to drop the whole matter. The real trouble, however, was that as the passion of war subsided the Allied peoples became more and more doubtful concerning the justice of the whole proceeding. Presently they were glad to have the trials provided for in the treaty forgotten. Conscience had reasserted its power.

Is it argued that this will not happen again? That this time there will be an international tribunal (administering what law?) from whose judgment none of the war criminals will be allowed to escape? It may prove so. But one notices no eagerness to bring Rudolf Hess to trial, even though Russia has demanded it. And not much is being said about trying Mussolini.

What, then, is the church's position on the treatment of Germany after Hitler's fall? Meeting as the certainty of victory emphasized the importance and near approach of that question, the Princeton Conference spoke with a prophetic insight which the victorious nations will disregard at their peril.

First acknowledging that concern for the future of 80,000,-000 Germans cannot be allowed to obscure or outweigh concern for the welfare of the 250,000,000 non-Germans in Europe, this Christian conference laid down these principles:

For the oppressed nations — victims of aggression — justice demands a restitution by Germany, but one that will not involve disintegration of the European economic structure.

For Germany — the aggressor — Christianity involves reconciliation on the basis of justice, and the meeting of a spirit of repentance with a spirit of forgiveness. This attitude must characterize all policies to which Christians lend support.

While the problem of Germany in the postwar period cannot be separated from its European setting, its solution must also take into account the wider objective — the early achievement of world organization embracing all nations. Our object should be to help Germany take her place within this organization, assuming all the responsibilities and rights which membership implies. With regard to the treatment of Germany, Christian principles must prevail. Controls and safeguards will be necessary. But it would be folly to attempt to apply repressive measures so vindictive and harsh that public opinion in the victor nations themselves will later revolt against them. This will inevitably bring about a breakdown of the peace structure and lead to renewed conflict.

" Restitution by Germany; reconciliation with Germany — the meeting of a spirit of repentance with a spirit of forgiveness." This is the proposal of the Christian church for postwar treatment of Germany. If this is not wisdom, then the church has no wisdom to offer groping men in these enigmatical days. But if the wisdom of the moral order is behind it, then to reject it will be to choose future suffering.

v

In the case of Japan, the same principles which the church has maintained should govern in the treatment of Germany must of course be observed. Despite the great bitterness of feeling on the part of some Americans toward the Japanese, there cannot be one wisdom to apply in Europe and another in Asia. The same moral order operates, laying the same interdict against the spirit of revenge and retaliation.

I confess that I am deeply disturbed by most of the books which are appearing these days dealing with the future in the Pacific. Almost without exception these are written by American journalists who claim the authority of first-hand investigation to support their recommendations. And almost without exception they call for war carried against Japan until all her cities have been laid waste, her people beggared, and a peace imposed which will never allow the rising generation to forget for a moment the awful consequences of defeat. Some of these writers seem to be trying to whip themselves into a state of sadistic fury; I note that some of the most furious are journalists who, before Pearl Harbor, were assuring the American people that a war with Japan would be child's play. The writer who is today more savage than all others in calling for the total destruction and permanent impoverishment of Japan was lecturing across the United States in the autumn of 1941 with promises that in war with this country Japan could not possibly hold out longer than sixty days.

Significantly enough, almost no such calls for revenge and retaliation come from China. The wisdom of more than four millenniums guards Chinese lips against such excess.

The Japanese problem is not a simple one. Japan has brutally mistreated the regions and people that have fallen into the hands of her army; justice demands that she make such restitution as is possible for all the human suffering she has caused. But the seventy million people of Japan must be afforded a future which contains some promise other than privation; otherwise they will become a constant source of intrigue and instability in the Orient. They are a hardy and a resourceful people, living in an island world which is almost destitute of the requisites of modern industrial life. Yet they have made their islands the most highly developed industrialized region of the Orient; in relation to the Asiatic mainland they stand today in much the same position that England occupied with relation to the European mainland a century ago.

Now these people are to be deprived of the territory they have seized, not alone in the present war but in colonial forays stretching back as far as to 1894. They are to be stripped of many sources of raw material which they have captured. They are to be denied the advantages of preferential position in many a teeming market. And then what is to be done with them? They will not starve in silence.

On the problem of Japan the Princeton Conference also spoke in terms which should rebuke the irresponsible hatemongering of those whose only cry is " Destroy! " The declaration does not go far toward outlining the specific provisions of the Far Eastern peace, but the principles which it lays down are clear. There should be no later confusion as to their application to specific problems of the postwar Orient:

Although the terms exacted from Japan will be severe, as Christians we urge that they be just, constructive and not retributive. They must not be carried to the point where Japan would be deprived of hope or prospect of economic revival and of readmission into international society with its consequent rights and duties.

Because the restoration of territories now occupied by Japan, notably Formosa, Korea and Manchuria, will inevitably deprive her of important features of the economy which she had built up before the war, steps must be taken (e.g., by providing access to markets for her exports and thus the means of obtaining foodstuffs and other vital materials, and by lending capital) to enable her to adjust her postwar economy to the legitimate welfare of her people without detriment to the economies of her neighbors.

In general, it will be neither possible nor desirable for the victorious powers to impose upon Japan conditions as to her future form of government; but they should shape their policy toward Japan so as to encourage the emergence within Japan of liberal and moderate elements disposed to cooperate in international arrangements for security, and other international projects of a global nature.

It is well to bear in mind that Chinese Christians participated in the formulation of that statement.

VI

If you could choose one page to be blotted out of the history of the United States, which would it be? Many thoughtful Americans, I am sure, would choose the page which bears the

record of the Reconstruction years after the Civil War. Probably nothing has left wounds so deep or has distilled so much
evil through our national life as that period in which, sure of
their own rectitude, men from the North persuaded themselves
that they were called of God to execute punishment on a South
that had been guilty of the sins of rebellion and slavery.

When I hear some of the wild cries for retribution against
our enemies today, I wonder at times whether those who thus
indulge their passions know nothing of their own national
history.

The responsibility of the Christian church to hold back the
tides of hate, the thirstings for revenge which may be loosed
at the end of the war, cannot be evaded. It is the testimony of
Mr. Lloyd George (as given in his *Memoirs of the Peace Conference*) that at Paris it was not, with few exceptions, the delegates who sought to write vengeance into the Treaty of
Versailles, but that the delegates were forced to bow to the demands for condign punishment which arose from the masses in
their home countries. It is the responsibility of the church to
see that no such unbridled passions destroy the coming effort
to write an enduring peace.

Up to this hour the governments have insisted that the Axis
nations can have peace only on the basis of unconditional surrender. They have made no engagements as to the treatment
which will be accorded those who have surrendered. As this
is being written, however, President Roosevelt has given this
personal assurance:

Except for the responsible Fascist leaders, the people of the Axis
need not fear unconditional surrender to the United Nations. I
have said that we shall bring food for the starving and medicine
for the sick in the areas liberated by the United Nations. We
have done so, under lend-lease, in North Africa. We are doing
so in Sicily. We shall continue to do so in other areas, as they
are liberated, to prevent economic breakdown and to aid the lib-

erated peoples to produce and to help themselves. We shall provide these necessary civilian supplies in support of our military operations and as a matter of simple humanity.

The people of Axis-controlled areas may be assured that when they agree to unconditional surrender they will not be trading Axis despotism for ruin under the United Nations. The goal of the United Nations is to permit liberated peoples to create a free political life of their own choosing and to attain economic security. These are two of the great objectives of the Atlantic Charter.[4]

This is the most hope-inspiring word for the future so far to come from a high source in the American or British governments. It serves as evidence that those governments are not beyond reach of the truth contained in the pronouncements of the Christian church on the postwar treatment of enemies. But it does not give the church a right to slumber. Voices will still be raised crying for retaliation, for revenge, for vengeance. While they are raised, the nature of the peace is in danger. While they are raised, it must be the business of the church to continue to proclaim its prophetic wisdom:

"Restitution where restitution is possible, but reconciliation everywhere — the meeting of a spirit of repentance with a spirit of forgiveness."

[4] From a letter transmitted to Congress by the President, August 25, 1943.

CHAPTER IX

HUNGER MEANS WAR

I

About a year ago there suddenly appeared in many American magazines one of the most remarkable advertisements ever published under commercial auspices. An aviation company must have spent hundreds of thousands of dollars in what advertising men call " double page spreads " to place before the American public a six-point postwar social and economic program drawn up by the Archbishop of Canterbury. After the war, said the Archbishop in this message carried to the public by so unusual a method, the industrial process must treat the consumer as its controlling end, rather than as a means to profit. To achieve the changes in the social order which this will require, these six immediate goals must be sought:

1. Every child should find itself a member of a family housed with dignity and decency, so that it may grow up in a happy fellowship unspoiled by underfeeding or overcrowding, by dirty and drab surroundings or by mechanical monotony in environment.

2. Every child should have the opportunity of an education until years of maturity. This education should be inspired by faith in God and find its focus in worship.

3. Every citizen should be secure in possession of such income as will enable him to maintain a home and bring up children in such conditions as are described in paragraph 1 above.

4. Every citizen should have a voice in the conduct of the business or industry which is carried on by means of his labor, and the satisfaction of knowing that his labor is directed to the well-being of the community.

5. After the war, every citizen should have sufficient daily lei-

sure, with two days of rest in seven, and an annual holiday with pay, to enable him to enjoy a full personal life.

6. Every citizen should have assured liberty in the forms of freedom of worship, of speech, of assembly and of association for special purposes.

Doubtless the publication of such an advertisement surprised some people. Who would expect an Archbishop — and an Archbishop of the Anglican Church at that! — to be talking about such matters? Perhaps it shocked others. Who would expect an Archbishop to be talking about such matters in this way? Why, that fourth point alone contains the seeds of a social revolution! Let Archbishops and all other Christian clergy, together with the churches which have ordained them, stick to their own business!

Those who talk in this way would probably be outraged to be told that the Christian church regards just such questions as the Archbishop discussed in that airways advertisement as peculiarly its business. It is no longer willing to remain silent concerning the conditions under which men must live or earn their livelihood. And its concern for men's social and economic opportunities is an integral part of its concern for peace. For it knows that as long as great numbers of men lack bread, or as long as they live in insecurity for themselves and hopelessness for their children, there can be no settled world order. Hunger means war.

Peace, therefore, is more than a matter of boundaries or armaments or military bases. Peace is a matter of food, employment, opportunity, social status. It is a matter of trade between nations. (" When goods cannot pass frontiers," Cordell Hull once said, " armies will.") It is a matter of doing away with the envy, the sense of frustration, the growing will to make trouble which comes when the people in a " have-not " nation look at what they regard as the opulence of the people in " have " countries. In the service of peace, the Christian church must stand in judgment on the social and economic order.

II

When it comes to preparation for postwar requirements, the slightest study will show that the social and economic problems which must be met are of two sorts — short-range and long-range. The short-range are those which must be dealt with from the instant firing ceases, to provide food and clothing and shelter for the millions facing death in war-ravaged lands. The long-range are those problems within the domestic and international economic order which must be solved if society itself is not to be an eternal battlefield.

As to short-range economic problems, perhaps enough has already been said in these pages. But there must be no repetition of the policy which the Allied nations pursued after the first World War, when a food blockade of Germany was continued for months after the Armistice. It may be doubted whether any other single factor did so much to embitter Germany. The whole business was a moral atrocity; every child who died from malnutrition in that post-Armistice blockade was as much a victim of barbarism as any soldier shot after surrender. As Winston Churchill has testified, in his book *The Aftermath*, it was the protest of the soldiers in Lord Plumer's army on the Rhine which finally forced the blockade's end.

One of the most disturbing rebuffs suffered by the church during the war has been the refusal of the Anglo-American governments to accede to its prayers for food for the population of occupied portions of Europe. The whole pitiful story need not be recounted here. Suffice it to say that responsible church quarters became convinced that food could be distributed to the women and children of lands overrun by the Axis under conditions which would insure it against falling into enemy hands; that the feeding undertaken in Greece, at the insistence of a highly important neutral, Turkey, was carried through without German interference or looting of supplies; that by the fall of 1942 an almost unanimous volume of church petition for such feeding was going up in the United States and Great Britain. But the Allied governments remained adamant.

This very failure to secure relief for some of the needy in Europe while the war continues will, however, increase the determination of the church to see that nothing holds up immediate succor after the Axis surrenders. This must be general; the first move must be to drive away the specter of starvation from every part of the Continent. Apparently, this is one policy on which the United Nations are truly united. They realize that, unless this work of instant relief is carried through, there can be no such social stability in the postwar Europe as will be required for the establishment of stable governments.

Of course, the immediate economic problem will not be simply that of feeding. The whole economic machine will have to be set to functioning again over much of the Continent. Factories must be rebuilt, and when rebuilt supplied with raw materials. Communication systems must be restored. Shelter must be provided for millions. Seed, fertilizer, farm machinery will be required before many countries can again grow their own food. Currencies are likely to be in chaos. All these things will require help. Credits must be furnished. Supplies must be made available. The ships and planes to carry these supplies to the places where they are needed will have to be provided. The days immediately after the fighting ends will see a race between rehabilitation and chaos in Europe.

III

But let us consider the long-term social and economic problem. This is not to be thought of in the comparatively simple terms of setting up certain machinery and adopting certain policies to deal with an emergency situation clear to every seeing eye. This long-range problem is hardly a problem of machinery at all, although to read some economists and sociologists one might think that it is. What is really involved is the need for far-reaching and fundamental change in the whole social and economic order. And that has far more to do with the motives which underlie that order, which make men function within it, than with any mere overhauling of the methods and agencies by which it functions.

In connection with the world crisis, no statement is more frequently heard than that we have come into a period of revolution. What is meant by such a term? As many use it, not much. It is for them simply an impressive polysyllable to drop into a speech or article. James Burnham is fully justified in the ridicule which, in his book *The Machiavellians*, he heaps on the highly paid minister who tells his wealthy congregation, " My friends, we are living in the midst of a world revolution," and then goes placidly on, leaving his hearers — and himself — as content and torpid as before.

But this *is* a period of revolution. Governments are being overthrown, but the overthrow of governments is not the revolution. The globe is circled by war, but the war is not the revolution. Great landed estates are being broken up and the luxuries of inherited wealth taken away by taxation, but such transfer of wealth is not the revolution. All these things, and many other phenomena which might be mentioned, are aspects of the revolution — its working out in the day-by-day actions of men. The revolution itself, however, is taking place at a deeper level.

This revolution in which the contemporary world finds itself involved marks the passing of laissez-faire capitalism as the governing social and economic faith in the dominant West. Its struggle grows out of the effort to substitute goals and motives for human action which differ, not in degree but in nature, from the goals and motives which have been acknowledged ever since the last great revolution, when feudalism faded from the scene. I do not have time here, nor is there need, to go over that demonstration, so well made by Troeltsch and Weber and Tawney, of the way in which the laissez-faire order developed out of the Renaissance and the Protestant Reformation. But it is that order, which has had such close relations with Protestantism, which is now ending its historic term and passing into limbo.

Three basic drives have motivated the laissez-faire order. The first was the drive for production; the second the drive for wealth; and the third the drive for human rights. All meshed together to produce what has been the most liberal — in the sense of liberating — and most prosperous order that Western man has known. Certain conditions have, to be sure, fostered this prosperity. The occupation of the Americas, the development of virgin sources of supplies and markets in Asia and Africa, gave laissez faire an opportunity without which its life-term must have been much shorter. There are still many of the sort who talk about a " return to the free market " who apparently fail to realize that the laissez-faire order has been doomed ever since the disappearance of the frontier and of unrestricted colonial exploitation. Such measure of that order as survives today, hedged with governmental and cartel restrictions and the demand for an end to the old colonialism, is no more than a walking corpse.

What the new order will be like when it is finally full grown, we may not yet be able to say. But there are indications all over the world of the change that is in process. Russia is one such indication. So is the New Deal in the United States. So has been the readiness of desperate people in Germany and Italy and elsewhere in Europe to desert the standards of liberal democracy and to rally to those of that betrayal of the revolutionary spirit — Fascism. It is in this sense that it is right to call the war a product of the revolution.

And what is the common core of ideas to be found in these separate manifestations? Surely it should not be difficult to discern. There is the determination, first, that the industrial machine shall be made to function to provide all men with the necessities of life — yes, and with more than the necessities. Since technology has made this possible, then morals and politics must see that it is achieved. This is the emphasis on the interest of the consumer as paramount for which the Archbishop of Canterbury calls. Second, there is the conviction that man's standing in society must be judged not by the wealth he amasses but by his contribution to the welfare of the total group. And third, and closely connected with the second, there is the belief that individual rights must be made subordinate to collective rights; that the obligations of the individual come before his exercise of rights. The dangers inherent in these two latter ideas have already been revealed by the rise of state totalitarian systems. But the need which is forcing their acceptance is to be seen in the individual irresponsibility which has brought the liberal democracies to the edge of the abyss.

Here is in truth a revolution which goes to the very roots of Western society. Work is to be primarily for consumption, not for the profits of production; social status is to be measured by contribution to the general welfare, not by riches; individual rights are to be subordinated to obligations, and community rights are to be paramount over all.

But what holds back the realization of this new order? What is required before the agony of this period when the new order is struggling to be born shall give place to the peace of its fulfillment?

In a passage of brilliant analysis in the book, *Conditions of Peace*, to which I have already referred, Edward Hallett Carr points out that the only condition under which man is now

ready to conduct his society on the basis of the three funda-
mentals outlined is in time of war. When war comes community rights are recognized as paramount, individual obligations take precedence over individual rights, the pursuit of
private wealth gives way to the furtherance of public welfare,
and the productive process is required to yield utmost consumption without regard to restrictions of private profit. But we
have not yet achieved a motivation which will yield the same
results in time of peace. The realization of the new social
order which our contemporary world revolution is seeking
waits on the discovery of that motivation.

In other words, Professor Carr leaves us with a moral crisis
on our hands. " There is no practical difficulty," he writes,
" about the solution of the economic problem: what we lack is
a sufficiently compelling moral purpose." And this moral
drive will come into being only when modern man finds a faith
that (1) will be affirmative rather than negative in spirit, striving to establish the good rather than centering its efforts on the
suppression of evil; (2) will win the loyalty of the " little
man " — the man who feels himself helpless in the grip of im-
personal economic forces and huge industrial combinations;
(3) will make the solution of economic problems its first responsibility; (4) will attack unemployment by the expansion
of needs and the creation of a moral imperative to meet those
needs; (5) will revive the idea of equality, essential to primitive Christianity but lost in the private profit-seeking of capitalism; (6) will stress individual obligations rather than rights;
(7) will stress the obligations of nations to the world community rather than national rights, and (8) will seek a new syn-
thesis in the ancient debate between the claims of liberty and
of authority.[1]

Where is this faith to come from? There may be varying
answers, but Professor Carr declares that there are only two

[1] Cf. *Conditions of Peace*, chapter 5.

movements or faiths whose universal principles and purposes
offer hope. These are Christianity and communism. Neither
as now functioning will be able to awaken in men the faith
which their social needs requires. But the promise is potential
in both. And Professor Carr does not dismiss the Christian
potentiality with the easy contempt which characterizes so
many secular observers. Rather he writes, in words which
should be productive of deep thought everywhere in the Christian church:

It would be a mistake to minimize the role played even today
in Western civilization by what are vaguely called " Christian
ideals " or " the Christian ethic." There is here a source of common feeling which, however obscure and inarticulate, helps to
keep in being an underlying sense of common values and of unity
between peoples. It is not inconceivable that the new leadership
for which the world craves may arise from within the Christian
church. But this hypothesis appears to presuppose a transformation of Christianity, or a revival of its primitive spirit, which
would in itself amount to a revolution. Those who believe that
a " return to Christianity " is the clue to our problems must face
the task of re-creating Christianity before they can use it as a
foundation on which to rebuild the world. . . . The cooperation
between the Western peoples and Soviet Russia in the war should
help to resolve the antithesis, incidental rather than fundamental,
between the secular ideals of Christianity and those of communism.[2]

IV

To what extent is this task of re-creating Christianity going
forward, and so bringing to life among Christians the operation of new motives which shall produce a new social and economic order in which men may live in lasting peace? Perhaps
to a greater extent than even so friendly an observer as Professor Carr knows. Certainly to a greater extent than is

[2] *Idem*, pages 120, 121.

recognized by the commonalty of mankind. In support of this claim, turn now to consideration of the Manifesto issued by the Malvern Conference and to the declaration on " The Economic Bases of a Just and Durable Peace" put forth by the Delaware Conference.

The Malvern Conference, as has been said, was made up of more than two hundred leading clerics and laymen of the Church of England, who met during the opening days of 1941. It confined its attention almost entirely to the ills which afflict the social order. In this its range of attention may seem narrower than that of Delaware. But Malvern proceeded on the assumption that, without a social order which makes possible domestic peace within the Western nations, there can be no hope of abiding international peace. Who shall say that its assumption was unsound?

In many respects these two gatherings — one drawn from a state church with hoary conservative traditions and a financial stake in the passing order and the other for the most part from communions jealous of their freedom — arrived at strikingly similar conclusions. Thus, both saw the war as a result of the breakdown of the old social order, Malvern casting its verdict in theological, and Delaware in moral and sociological, terms. Said Malvern:

The war is not to be regarded as an isolated evil detached from the general conditions of Western civilization during the last period. Rather it is to be seen as one symptom of a widespread disease and maladjustment resulting from loss of conviction concerning the reality and character of God, and the true nature and destiny of man.

And said Delaware:

We are convinced that the present struggle of the nations is not just another war in the history of mankind. It is the upheaval of the old order and the birth of a new. The relationships of men will never again be the same, nor should they be the same, for they have not been founded on the eternal truths of God.

With prophetic boldness both church conferences proclaimed the shortcomings and consequent doom of the Western social and economic order. The line runs straight from Amos at Bethel to the representatives of the Christian church making this declaration at Delaware:

We are deeply disturbed by the economic distress of millions of our fellow men and by economic conditions that threaten the extension of the Kingdom of God on earth.

We view the economic tensions and distresses of our day as symptoms of a general world disorder. In our era production has been carried on primarily with a view to monetary gains. Profit has been the principal incentive relied upon to turn the wheels of industry and to bring forth the fruits of the soil. . . .

Any economic program which allows the quest for private gain to disregard human welfare, which regiments human beings and denies them freedom of collective bargaining, thus reducing labor to a mere commodity; any program which results in mass unemployment or dire poverty in mine or factory or farm; any program which fails to conserve natural resources and results in soil deterioration and erosion and along with it human erosion and deterioration of rural life in home and school and church, is manifestly wrong.

Against such evils the church should arouse the conscience of mankind in every nation. The church must demand economic arrangements measured by human welfare as revealed by secure employment, decent homes and living conditions, opportunity for youth, freedom of occupation and of cultural activities, recognition of the rights of labor, and security in illness and old age. To secure these arrangements it must appeal to the Christian motive of human service as paramount to personal or governmental coercion.

And Malvern? Well, the high point came at Malvern when the young Member of Parliament, Sir Richard Acland, introduced his now-famous "Amendment," which, after vigorous debate, the presiding Archbishop announced as adopted *nemine contradicente*. Can this be the voice of an established church? Here, in part, is the Acland Amendment:

There is no structural organization of society which can bring about the coming of the Kingdom of God on earth, since it is a gift of God, and since all systems can be perverted by the selfishness of man. Therefore, the church as such can never commit itself to any proposed change in the structure of society as being a self-sufficient means of salvation.

But the church can point to those features of our existing society which, while they can never prevent individual men and women from becoming Christian, are contrary to divine justice, and act as stumbling-blocks, making it harder for men to lead Christian lives.

In our present civilization we believe that the maintenance of that part of the structure of our society, by which the ultimate ownership of the principal industrial resources of the community can be vested in the hands of private owners, may be such a stumbling-block. On the one hand it may deprive the poorest members of the community of the essentials of life. On the other, while these resources can be so owned, men will strive for their ownership for themselves. As a consequence, a way of life founded on the supremacy of the economic motive will remain, which is contrary to God's plan for mankind.

For one or both of these reasons, the time has come for Christians to proclaim the need for striving toward a form of society in which, while the essential value of the individual human personality is preserved, the continuance of these abuses will be no longer possible.

May I be permitted a comment or two at this point which might perhaps be regarded as an extended footnote? The sensational, not to say revolutionary, nature of this pronouncement, coming from a conference of leaders of the established Church of England, hardly needs to be pointed out. When these Anglican leaders adopted it, they undoubtedly knew that it would stir up a storm in secular quarters. It did. Columns in the British press were given to denouncing the Archbishops and all churchmen for meddling in matters which were none of their business. It is possible that this press storm blew to more violent proportions than the Malvern delegates anticipated. At any rate, when the Malvern Manifesto reached the public, a small but significant change had been edited into the Acland Amendment. In the sentence in the third paragraph, as printed above, which refers to private ownership of the principal industrial resources of the community as a stumbling-block to the leading of a Christian life, the word " is " had been changed to " may be." Malvern actually voted that " ownership of the principal industrial resources of the community . . . in the hands of private owners *is* such a stumbling-block." The document was sent out, and it is here printed, declaring that such private ownership " *may be* such a stumbling-block." [3]

In the light of all the courage shown by Malvern, and its leaders, in wrestling with the problems of contemporary society, it may be unfair to accuse them of having been frightened into a watered-down declaration in this instance by the baying of the press. But the phenomenon is not unknown in church gatherings, and when it occurs it always represents a betrayal of prophetic responsibility. There are ministers whose highest conception of success in their calling is to get two or three inches of commendatory mention in the columns of the secular press. There are church leaders who tremble in their shoes

[3] Also lost somewhere between the adjournment of the Malvern Conference and the publication of its Manifesto, which had the editorial supervision of Dr. Temple, then Archbishop of York, was this resolution: " Whatever may be the necessities of the period immediately following the war, our aim must be the unification of Europe as a cooperative commonwealth, first in common effort for the satisfaction of general need, and secondly in such political institutions as express the common purpose and facilitate its development."

at the thought that a church gathering, intent on discharging its prophetic function, might say anything which the newspapers might "misunderstand," and which might draw unfavorable headlines or editorials. Let but some newspaper — blind in its partisanship, parochial in its outlook, tied hand and foot to the profit-seeking order, often drawing a large part of its revenues from commodities which spread ruin through society — let but some such paper begin to rumble, or even let it be but feared that it may begin to rumble, and there is a certain type of church "leadership" which could not be induced to join the legendary Coolidge pastor in coming out against sin. This fear of the press does tragic damage to the work of the church today, and the Christian ministry will never measure up to its high calling until it gets over it.

The other comment I wish to make on the Acland Amendment concerns the proofs of sincerity given by its authors. Church gatherings have been known to utter brave words without much intention of putting them to the test. Malvern sought to establish its own sincerity by resolving that "Christians, clergy and laity alike, cannot take part in this work" — the work of bringing into being a new form of society — "unless they are ready to advocate and bring about a complete change in the internal financial position of the Church of England." And Sir Richard Acland sought to meet his own test, after Malvern, by returning to the nation the more than thirty thousand acres of revenue-producing land which had come into his possession from a long line of baronial forebears and by founding the Common Wealth party which would transform England into a socialist state.

Faced by such a requirement for a new social order, with new goals and new motives, how should the church go forward? Delaware's declaration reads:

In a day when traditional revolutionary upheavals have swept away the traditional economic organization in Russia, Italy and

Germany, and now when, by reason of the necessities of war, that economic order is being radically reorganized everywhere, the church has a manifest duty in the economic field, both urban and rural. That duty is not to line up on the side of any economic system and certainly not to prescribe details or advocate panaceas. Its responsibility lies in a deeper moral realm. As Christians we must be vitally concerned for the preservation of human values in any and every system. The Christian doctrine of man as a child of God carries with it the demand that all men, without distinction of race, creed or class, shall be afforded the economic means of life and growth.

And then the Delaware Conference, lest its disavowal of a desire to " prescribe details " of the changes it sought in the social and economic order be misunderstood, went ahead to list the nine specific recommendations which will be found on pages 207 and 208 of the Appendix in this book. These recommendations it presented as in a sense a commentary on this statement of general principle:

The building of a just and peaceful world involves the building of national and local communities on the basis of justice, freedom and cooperation for the common good.

We believe that a new ordering of economic life is both imminent and imperative, and that it will come either through voluntary cooperation within the framework of democracy or through explosive political revolution. We recognize the need of experimentation with various forms of ownership and control, private, cooperative and public. It is hardly to be supposed that any one system, whether of private, cooperative or public enterprise, is suited to all kinds of production, distribution and service. The production and distribution of goods on the basis of voluntary cooperation is an experiment which in many parts of the world is meeting with notable success.

At this point, Malvern was even more specific. Since " the proper purpose of work is the satisfaction of human needs," it declared that " Christian doctrine has insisted that production exists for consumption." There goes the whole system of production for profit, right out the church's window! It held, moreover, that man must no longer be simply a cog in the machine. The " status of man as man, independently of the economic process, must find expression in the managerial framework of industry; the rights of labor must be recognized as in principle equal to those of capital in the control of industry, whatever the means by which this transformation is effected."

And finally, this blast: " It is a traditional doctrine of Christendom that property is necessary to fulness of personal life; all citizens should be enabled to hold such property as contributes to more independence and spiritual freedom without impairing that of others; but where the rights of property conflict with the establishment of social justice or the general social welfare, those rights should be overridden, modified, or, if need be, abolished." If you question whether the prophetic fire still burns in the Christian church, read those last words again: " Where the rights of property conflict with the establishment of social justice or the general social welfare, those rights should be overridden, modified, or, if need be, abolished." Malvern — a conference of leaders of the Church of England — speaking!

V

The future of the international economic order did not, as has been said, fall within the purview of Malvern.[4] Had it done so, that conference would surely have applied with equal rigor the principles which it avowed for reconstitution of domestic society. But Delaware, dealing with the total problem of future peace, could not be silent. Among its Guiding Principles it had laid down this:

---

[4] Malvern did, however, register its opinion that " the system under which we have lived has been a predisposing cause of war, even though those who direct and profit by it have desired peace." The inference is clear.

We believe that economic security is no less essential than political security to a just and durable peace. Such security nationally and internationally involves among other things the use of material resources and the tools of production to raise the general standard of living. Nations are not economically self-sufficient, and the natural wealth of the world is not evenly distributed. Accordingly the possession of such natural resources should not be looked upon as an opportunity to promote national advantage or to enhance the prosperity of some at the expense of others. Rather such possession is a trust to be discharged in the general interest. This calls for more than an offer to sell to all on equal terms. Such an offer may be a futile gesture unless those in need can, through the selling of their own goods and services, acquire the means of buying. The solution of this problem, doubtless involving some international organization, must be accepted as a responsibility by those who possess natural resources needed by others.

Delaware had only praise for foreign economic policies inaugurated by the United States in the negotiation of the reciprocal trade acts, the measures taken to assure the economic stability of Latin American states, and particularly in the provision written into Article 7 of the Anglo-American lend-lease pact, calling for " postwar participation, by all countries of like mind, directed to the expansion, by appropriate international and domestic measures, of production, employment and exchanging consumption of goods which are the material foundations of the liberty and welfare of all peoples; to the elimination of all forms of discriminatory treatment in international commerce and to the reduction of tariffs and other trade barriers."

Delaware also gave its approval to the provisions of the fourth, fifth and sixth clauses of the Atlantic Charter:

Fourth, they will endeavor, with due respect to their existing obligations, to further the enjoyment by all states, great and small, victor and vanquished, of access, on equal terms, to the trade and to the raw materials of the world which are needed for their economic prosperity.

Fifth, they desire to bring about the fullest collaboration between all nations in the economic field with the object of securing, for all, improved labor standards, economic adjustment, and social security.

Sixth, after the final destruction of the Nazi tyranny they hope to see established a peace which will afford to all nations the means of dwelling in safety within their own boundaries and which will afford assurance that all men in all the lands may live out their lives in freedom from want and fear.

But while this church conference gave its general approval to these formulations, it had no illusions regarding their limitations as a charter for the international economic order which must be established after the war if peace is to endure. The joker in that fourth clause, " with due respect to their existing obligations," could hardly be overlooked, and Delaware did not overlook it. It asked Britain and the United States to get rid of any obligations which would block the fulfillment of the promise in the rest of the clause.

This church body recognized that the labor gains, promised in the fifth article, would never be achieved without some international collaboration in the control of economic life. Accordingly, it approved and asked more power for the International Labor Organization. And it knew that in the long run the peace of national borders, pictured in the sixth declaration, depends on the freedom with which trade can cross those borders. So the conference called for " the progressive elimination of restrictions on world trade, such as tariffs and quotas, under the guidance of an international organization and by other appropriate methods."

That is only a part of the recommendations dealing with the future organization of society, internationally as well as nationally, adopted by the Delaware Conference. Perhaps the reader who studies carefully each section in the economic division of the Delaware report, as it appears on pages 205 to 209 of the Appendix, will discover there material even more revolutionary in its social implications than any I have quoted. But surely enough has been said to show that, at both Malvern and Delaware, prophetic utterances on the nature of the social order have been formulated. The Christian church has only to stand by them and insistently press them home in the minds of contemporary men to become the greatest force for change in this period of revolution.

VI

But there are breakers ahead. Newspapers will howl; some laymen will threaten to withhold their largesse; ministers will find their wealthy parishioners looking at them askance. The war will exhaust the energies, perhaps of a whole generation. After it is over, most of the men and women who have come through its perils will for a time have no desire for other battles. There will be the same natural wish to relax for a while, to "return to normalcy," that lost the peace after the last war. Already, with the first signs of sure victory, this swing toward the old paths has set in.

Mr. Wallace is derided for suggesting that Hottentots deserve to have milk. Mr. Welles takes his tall talk about the liberation of all peoples with him into exile from the government. Mr. Willkie is exhorted, if he wants another nomination, to forget about collaboration with China and Russia and other nations overseas and to come out for good old G.O.P. traditionalism. The Beveridge plan is shelved in London; the NRPB plan is shelved in Washington. Farmers and business are visibly moving toward alliance to block the ambitions of labor.

How far we are in actuality from putting into practice the principles which the Christian church advocates has already been shown in the case of the dismal fate of all proposals to eliminate racial discrimination from American immigration and naturalization laws. It is shown with equal clarity by the fate of a proposal, originally made by John Foster Dulles, which would have taken a first, tiny, faltering step toward a recognition of international brotherhood in the realm of foreign trade policy.

A year or two before America was plunged into the war Mr. Dulles, who is the chairman of the Federal Council's Commission to Study the Bases of a Just and Durable Peace, thought that the time had come to do something to mitigate America's complete and brusque exercise of absolute sovereignty in matters relating to international trade. Mr. Dulles, who has participated as an American delegate in many international conferences — including the Paris Peace Conference — and is a New York corporation lawyer, is too old a hand at the political game to attempt much as a beginning. But he succeeded in having introduced into Congress a resolution which provided that, in case any legislation were under consideration which any foreign government might allege would, in case of adoption, do it economic harm, Congress would hold hearings to determine the truth or falsity of that claim. That was all! There was no promise to amend the pending legislation or in any other way to seek to assuage the feelings of the protesting nation. There was simply a proposal to hold hearings before this government took any economic action which might damage anyone else. That resolution still slumbers in some committee's archives; from that day to this it has been impossible to induce Congress so much as to consider it!

It is a salutary thing to recall such a fact lest the church deceive itself as to the magnitude of the task it undertakes when it calls for a new order of society, both domestic and international. Simply adopting Malvern and Delaware reports, however prophetic in their content, will not save man from the disaster toward which his society is headed. The church must give contemporary man no rest. Weary though he may be of struggle, tragically as he may have burned away his energies in warfare, still the church must insist that he listen when it says that the present social order, judged by all Christian standards and by the moral law, is immoral; that it must be changed fundamentally or man can never live at peace.

CHAPTER X

HOME TO THE CITY OF GOD

I

Not long ago I watched a technicolor film unfold a record of the advance of American forces across North Africa, as they moved into position for the later campaign in Tunisia. The picture hardly compared with those taken by the Russians and the British on their fighting fronts. Nevertheless, the very names of the places mentioned must have given it unusual interest to those at all familiar with the history which has been made during the long centuries along the southern shore of the Mediterranean.

As I watched, there flashed on the screen a beautiful harbor, with transports standing offshore while heavily freighted lighters and crowded landing barges pushed their way to the quays. The Americans, said the voice of the commentator, were taking possession of Bone.

At once I was in another world. It was not 1943, but about the year 426. The name of the city was not then Bone, but Hippo. The great metropolis to the east was not Tunis, but Carthage. Yet it was likewise a time of invasion. The order which Rome had imposed upon the Western world for centuries was being shattered. Hordes of ferocious men from the forests of northern Europe had poured through the passes of the Alps and Pyrenees into southern Europe. And on the walls of Hippo an old man stood looking westward toward the narrow straits at the Pillars of Hercules, across which would soon come the invading army of the Vandals, to sack the city and smash into the dust the whole civilization in that garden region of what had been the proud empire.

The old man knew the fate in store for his city and for his countrymen. He heard also the murmurs which surrounded him. This destruction, so close at hand, he could hear it whispered, came as punishment for desertion of the old gods, the old ways. Men had been betrayed by the enticements of a new faith. Now, in the hour of their need, it could offer no help wherewith to withstand the advancing armies of Genseric. Would it not have been better if this new faith had never been allowed to penetrate the territories of the empire, sapping its strength? Were not Nero and Domitian and the other Caesars who sought to exterminate it right?

Slowly the old man climbed down from the city walls and made his way through the narrow, crowded streets, back to the bishop's palace. His head bent in thought, he went directly to the library, where pages of manuscript covered his table. And there, having come straight from the presence of an encompassing destruction, he wrote the final words of what men were to cherish as one of the handful of books which live through the ages. For the old Bishop of Hippo who heard those murmurs and faced that destroying host of Vandals was, of course, St. Augustine. And the book which he wrote in the very hour of an empire's fall was the immortal *De Civitate Dei* — " The City of God."

What has given Augustine's book immortality? It is the philosophy of history which he worked out in the imagery of the two cities. There is, he said, a City of Earth, and there is a City of God. The City of Earth is that secular city, based on the love of self, which, while it serves for a time to preserve order, is always under sentence of destruction, is always in process of passing away. But the City of God is the heavenly city, given visible form in the Christian church. It is based on the love of God, which is the denial of self. It stands no matter what else falls. It lives no matter what else dies. It grows no matter what else passes away. It has a wisdom which is not of this world, but which is eternal. Within its walls there is salvation. It is a city which is not in the far-away heavens, though it is in the heavens, but a city whose reality is immanent in the earthly city and whose life and destiny are to be worked out on earth. " Thy Kingdom come on earth! " Hence it becomes, in the hour when man is most dismayed, the home of every soul seeking truth and certainty.

Sitting there looking at that film, punctuated now by the flash of guns and the explosion of falling bombs, while the wild scream of the dive-bomber shrieked an infernal obbligato, I found myself wondering whether there might not be something symbolic in the fact that our eyes were being directed back to Bone . . . to Hippo . . . to St. Augustine . . . to the City of God. May not the time be at hand when men, seeing the pride of the City of Earth humbled in the doom which its own self-seeking has brought to pass, will turn again to the City of God? May not the very horror and disintegration which surround them in the City of Earth open their minds to the truth which is the possession of the City of God?

Are not men beginning to ask, as the men of the Roman Empire were asking in that fifth century, whether the secular order has lost its moral power, whether its own folly has brought it under sentence of dissolution? If the arrangements made between the nations at the close of this present conflict again destroy the hope of lasting peace, again grasp at a momentary advantage heedless of the sure future penalty, will not men in their disillusionment be ready at last to listen to the accents of the prophetic voice, speaking the wisdom of the unchanging moral order? Then may it not be that the hour is at hand when harried, baffled, desperate man will turn homeward to the City of God?

II

No words of mine are required to prove that the world is at a crisis. Thoughtful men see the evidence everywhere, and even those who are least introspective feel the gathering tragedy in their bones. The issue which confronts them can be put very simply, in two questions that can no longer be denied: Can the world make peace? Or will it plunge on into chaos?

Because the prospects are so dark, men everywhere find their hope fading, their fear rising. But the Christian church says that there can be peace — peace now when the fighting ceases, and peace to last for long generations. It says that man can make peace as soon as he will forsake the idolatries of an order in which he worshiped himself, his own wisdom, his own wealth, to turn to the worship of the true God. Or, as the Christians at Malvern put it: "God himself is the sovereign of all human life; all men are his children, and ought to be brothers of one another; through Christ the Redeemer, they can become what they ought to be."

Begin there, says the Christian church. Do not begin where the Caesar begins, where the politician begins, where the opportunist begins. Do not begin in any compromise, but begin with truth, with the eternal truth, with the truth of God and man's relation to him. Believe that. Live by that. Then go on to work out the relations of society, in all their national and international aspects, in the light of that, and all will follow. *All* — a new worth for individual living, a new reward for the processes of labor, a new stability for the state, a new mutuality among the races, lasting peace! All will follow because men who thus worship the true God will be devoted to the service of justice.

In our dire need we say that we seek security. There is no security but the security of justice. We say we seek international and interracial understanding. There is no understand-

ing but the understanding of justice. We say we seek peace.
There is no peace but the peace of justice.

What is justice? The question baffles us as it has baffled men
for countless generations. When profound students of the
human heart tell us that there can be no perfect justice among
such sinful men as we are, we know that to be so. But man's
moral sense enables him to see the direction in which justice
lies. And we know that a far closer approximation to justice
than we have attained (or sought) in the past — what the great
Aquinas has called "rough justice" — is within the compass of
our achievement. At the very least, we can greatly lessen the
area of injustice as between man and man, as between nation
and nation, as between race and race.

It is to spur us to that attempt that the prophetic church
lifts its voice.

III

Is it objected that the secular order will not listen? That
the state, the privileged classes, the hitherto dominating racial
groups, while they protest their devotion to peace and their
desire for peace, will not seek peace on the terms which the
Christian church lays down, nor consider paying the price
which it would demand? Is it said that the church will be derided as impractical, visionary, stultifyingly perfectionist?

What of it?

In the first place, the charge is not true. It has been one
purpose of this book to show that practically every condition
laid down by the Christian church as the price of just and lasting peace has the agreement, the approval of men who live at
the very center of 'practical' affairs. The truth which the
church proclaims as a prophetic insight from its worship of the
true God and its apprehension of the moral order he has created, is the same truth which these men have learned in the
school of experience.

And in the second place, the responsibility of the church is not to the response of the secular order. Suppose the state will not hear. Suppose the privileged insist upon hugging to themselves their privileges. Suppose they all join in derision, or in heaping reproaches upon the church. What matter? There will be sorrow for the blindness of men's eyes and the hardness of their hearts. But the church has only one duty — to remain true to its own best insight. What that gives it to speak, it must speak. The result is in the hands of God.

IV

And what about man, dogged with the frustration of his disillusionment? He may stand in danger of losing faith in all his other institutions, but if he sees the church calm in the knowledge that it serves a living God, sure of the way of peaceful order which it has to offer, beleaguered man may respond to that; he may turn to that.

The world today bears striking resemblance to the world which St. Augustine knew. It seems indeed

> a darkling plain
> Swept with confused alarms of struggle and flight,
> Where ignorant armies clash by night.

But that is the world of the City of Earth. There is another world — the world that now exists within the City of God; the world which the church declares may finally displace that in which disillusioned man now finds himself. It is a world wherein there is far more to which to be true than " one another." It is a world wherein man is true to the living God, the Father who has revealed his purpose for man in Jesus Christ. There, within the world of the City of God, despairing man may come, to find his disillusionment vanished, to find himself living in an order of faith, hope and love.

APPENDIX

PROPOSALS OF PROTESTANT AND ROMAN CATHOLIC LEADERS OF GREAT BRITAIN

On December 21, 1940, the Archbishops of Canterbury and York, Arthur Cardinal Hinsley, Roman Catholic Archbishop of Westminster, and Walter H. Armstrong, Moderator of the Free Church Federal Council, put forward joint proposals for the consideration of statesmen after the war. The Ten Proposals are:

1. Extreme inequality of wealth should be abolished.
2. Every child, regardless of race or class, should have equal opportunities for education suitable to its peculiar capacities.
3. The family as a social unit must be safeguarded.
4. The sense of a divine vocation must be restored to man's daily work.
5. Resources of the earth should be used as God's gifts for the whole human race and used with due consideration for the needs of present and future generations.
6. The right to life and independence of all nations, large, small, strong or weak, must be safeguarded.
7. Disarmament must be mutually accepted, organic and progressive, in both letter and spirit.
8. International institutions must be created or recast to insure the loyal and faithful execution of international agreements.
9. Real needs and just demands of nations and peoples should be benevolently examined.
10. A peace settlement must be dictated by a sense of acute responsibility which weighs human statutes according to the holy, unshakable rules of divine law.[1]

THE MALVERN MANIFESTO

We, being members of the Church of England assembled in conference at Malvern from January 7 to 10, 1941, after seeking the guidance of the Holy Spirit, and having given the best consideration that we could to the present crisis of civilization, are generally agreed upon the following propositions.

---

[1] The last five proposals represent a summary of the five points on conditions of a just and honorable peace laid down by Pope Pius XII in a speech delivered on December 24, 1939.

The Disease of Civilization

1. The war is not to be regarded as an isolated evil detached from the general conditions of Western civilization during the last period. Rather it is to be seen as one symptom of a widespread disease and maladjustment resulting from loss of conviction concerning the reality and character of God, and the true nature and destiny of man. Accordingly we endorse the ten points put forward as Foundations of Peace by the two Anglican Archbishops, the Cardinal Archbishop of Westminster, and the Moderator of the Evangelical Free Church Council; we urge all Christian people to study those points and to support only such policies in the spheres concerned as tend to give effect to them. (See Appendix I.)

The Right of the Church to Speak

2. Because the church is not an association of men gathered together by the act of their own wills, but is a creation of God in Jesus Christ, through which as his Body Christ carries on his work for men, it has the duty and the right to speak, not only to its members, but to the world concerning the true principles of human life.

The Church in Its Own Life

3. The first, and if fully understood the whole, duty of the church is truly to be the church — the community of the Holy Spirit drawing men and nations into itself; that they may become sharers in its God-given life and so fulfill their several destinies according to God's purpose.

4. The church as we know it does not manifest this life of true community. We therefore urge that enterprises be initiated whereby that life can be made manifest.

Christians in Public Service

5. Christian people should take the fullest possible share in public life, both in Parliament, in municipal councils, in employers' and workers' organizations, and all other bodies affecting the public welfare, and constantly seek ways of expressing Christian principles through these channels.

THE CHURCH AND THE SOCIAL ORDER

(a) Resolution Adopted by the Conference Nemine Contradicente

6. God himself is the sovereign of all human life; all men are his children, and ought to be brothers of one another; through Christ the Redeemer they can become what they ought to be.

There can be no advance towards a more Christian way of life except through a wider and fuller acceptance of this faith, and through the adoption, by individuals, of the way of living which it implies.

There is no structural organization of society which can bring about the coming of the Kingdom of God on earth, since it is a gift of God, and since all systems can be perverted by the selfishness of man. Therefore, the church as such can never commit itself to any proposed change in the structure of society as being a self-sufficient means of salvation.

But the church can point to those features of our existing society which, while they can never prevent individual men and women from becoming Christian, are contrary to divine justice, and act as stumbling-blocks, making it harder for men to live Christian lives.

In our present civilization we believe that the maintenance of that part of the structure of our society, by which the ultimate ownership of the principal industrial resources of the community can be vested in the hands of private owners, may be such a stumbling-block. On the one hand it may deprive the poorest member of the community of the essentials of life. On the other, while these resources can be so owned, men will strive for their ownership for themselves. As a consequence, a way of life founded on the supremacy of the economic motive will remain, which is contrary to God's plan for mankind.

For one or both of these reasons, the time has come for Christians to proclaim the need for striving towards a form of society in which, while the essential value of the individual human personality is preserved, the continuance of these abuses will be no longer possible.

Christians, clergy and laity alike, cannot take part in this work unless they are ready to advocate and bring about a complete change in the internal financial position of the Church of England.

(b) Propositions Accepted in the Way Described Above
The General Principle

7. We fully endorse the following declarations of the Madras Conference: " It is not enough to say that if we change the individual we will of necessity change the social order. That is a half-truth. For the social order is not entirely made up of individuals now living. It is made up of inherited attitudes which have come down from generation to generation through customs, laws, institutions, and these exist in large measure independently of individuals now living. Change those individuals and you do not necessarily change the social order unless you organize those changed individuals into collective action in wide-scale frontal attack upon those corporate evils."

It should not be necessary to say that such a view as this does not in any way minimize the crucial significance of personal religion, which must always be the spring of Christian life.

Evangelism

8. The church has a testimony to the world. This is first and foremost testimony to the gospel itself; there is urgent need for more evangelistic preaching which may call men and women to submit their lives to Christ.

There is also need to create in all who are or become members of the church a sense of its world-wide mission and its world-wide fellowship.

The Christian Doctrine of Man

9. But the church has also a special testimony to the world in respect of its social and economic life. The Christian doctrine of man as created and redeemed by God for eternal fellowship with himself supplies on the one side the only sure foundation of freedom and of justice, and also on the other hand requires that men shall have an opportunity to become the best of which they are capable and shall find in the prosecution of their daily tasks fulfillment and not frustration of their human nature. This involves in our own time such an adjustment of machine production as to secure that the use and service of machinery may be a true vocation. The Christian doctrine of man as a child of God carries with it the sacredness of human personality; a civilization or social order must be judged by the extent to which it recognizes this in practice.

Sin: the Perversion of Man's True Purpose

10. Because we have neglected the true end of man, we have lost the controlling principle which allots to human activities their proper sphere and due relations to one another. Consequently, in the last period the economic activity of man, of which the product is the means to the good life rather than the good life itself, has become predominant, as though to produce material wealth were man's true end. We have here an example of the pervasive influence of human sin which the church must always keep before the minds and consciences of men. This is as relevant to schemes of reform to be operated by sinful men as to our judgment of the situation in which we find ourselves.

The Right to Property and the Rights of Property

11. It is a traditional doctrine of Christendom that property is necessary to fullness of personal life; all citizens should be enabled to hold such property as contributes to more independence and spiritual freedom without impairing that of others; but where the rights of property conflict with the establishment of social justice or the general social welfare, those rights should be overridden, modified or, if need be, abolished.

The Proper Purpose of Production

12. The proper purpose of work is the satisfaction of human needs; hence Christian doctrine has insisted that production exists for consumption; but man is personal in all his activities and should find in the work of production a sphere of truly human activity, and the doing of it should be for the producer a part of the "good life" and not only his way of earning a livelihood.

13. The existing industrial order, with the acquisitive temper character-

istic of our society, tends to recklessness and sacrilege in the treatment of natural resources. It has led to the impoverishment of the agricultural community, and is largely responsible for the problem of the "mass man," who is conscious of no status, spiritual or social, who is a mere item in the machinery of production, and who easily develops the herd psychology, which is automatically responsive to skillful propaganda.

A Challenge to Present Practice

14. The following propositions were laid before the conference, which regarded them as a serious challenge and desired that they should be further discussed in a committee containing economists, industrialists and representatives of labor:

(i) The industrial world as we know it offends at many points against the principles which we have affirmed. To a large extent production is carried on not to supply the consumer with goods but to bring profits to the producer; and the producer in turn is often subordinated to the purely financial ends of those who own the capital plant or supply the credit to erect or work it.

(ii) This method of ordering industry, which tends to treat human work and human satisfaction alike as means to a false end — namely, monetary gain — becomes a source of unemployment at home and dangerous competition for markets abroad. We have seen the unemployment of Germany cured by an armament program, whether adopted primarily for this purpose or not, and have cured our own, though (even so) not completely, by the same means. The system under which we have lived has been a predisposing cause of war, even though those who direct and profit by it have desired peace.

(iii) The monetary system should be so administered that what the community can produce is made available to the members of the community, the satisfaction of human needs being accepted as the only true end of production.

(iv) This status of man as man, independently of the economic process, must find expression in the managerial framework of industry; the rights of labor must be recognized as in principle equal to those of capital in the control of industry, whatever the means by which this transformation is effected.

(v) In international trade, a genuine interchange of mutually needed commodities must take the place of a struggle for a so-called favorable balance.

Conclusion

15. To sum up, we believe that the most vital demands to be made by the church with a view to social reconstruction are two: The restoration of man's economic activity to its proper place as the servant of his whole personal life; and the expression of his status in the natural world as a child of God for whom Christ died.

PRACTICAL RECOMMENDATIONS

1. The Life of the Church

(a) There is urgent need that the Church of England should radically reorganize its own economic and administrative system, and so reconstruct this as to make it an expression of unity of purpose and especially of brotherhood in the ministry. Until it does this, its testimony to the world will be blunted. Our sincerity in putting forward our other proposals will be judged, and rightly judged, by the energy with which we take this task in hand.

(b) Where possible, the whole congregation habitually worshiping together should regularly meet to plan and carry out some common enterprise, however simple, for the upbuilding of its community life and for the general good; if there are social evils in the locality, such as bad housing or malnutrition, or, at the present time, lack of air-raid shelters or bad conditions in those provided, or dearth of rations to which the people are entitled, let them consider how the evil can be remedied, either by securing the enforcement of existing laws or in other ways.

(c) In other places, let "cells" be formed upon the basis of common prayer, study and service. Groups should be formed wherever possible of people not ready as yet to join in Christian devotion, but who come together to study and discuss what is the Christian way of life for them and for society. In all such schemes the Christian people of a district belonging to various denominations should work together in close and friendly cooperation, and should all combine to foster true neighborliness in the community.

(d) The church might further encourage the development of ways and means, whether through membership of a Third Order or otherwise, which would enable men and women to live under a definite discipline and rule whilst following the ordinary professions of life.

2. The Order of Society

(a) Human status ought not to depend upon the changing demands of the economic process; no one should be deprived of the support necessary for the "good life" by the fact that there is at some time no demand for his labor.

(b) The church should strive to keep alive in all men and in all functional groups a sense of vocation by constantly calling upon them to consider what is the purpose of their various activities, and to keep this true to the purpose of God for his people.

(c) In all that is planned, regard must be paid to the family as, by God's appointment, the basic social unit on whose stability and welfare all other social welfare in large measure depends.

(d) In like manner we must recover reverence for the earth and its resources, treating it no longer as a reservoir of potential wealth to be exploited, but as a storehouse of divine bounty on which we utterly depend. This will carry with it a deliberate revival of agriculture, both by securing to the agricultural laborer good wages and to the farmer a secure and just price. We regard this as indispensable to the true balance of the national life.

(e) The restoration of agriculture must be utilized for the revival of true community, which is possible in a village as it is not in great cities. Here something can be done to start the movement away from mass psychology towards the development of personality in fellowship.

(f) We urge that use be made of the opportunity provided by the presence of so many citizens of other countries in our own to make personal friendships with them and to learn more fully to understand the outlook of those nations. Recognizing the gravity of the Jewish problem, we urge all Christians to take their part in seeking an effective solution even at real cost, and in all circumstances to check the growth of anti-Semitic passions.

(g) We regard as of primary importance the securing to all children and adolescents the educational opportunities best suited to develop their faculties and to enable them to take their full share as Christian citizens in the life of the community — spiritual, cultural, economic.

(h) This involves securing for all children effective Christian teaching given by teachers desiring and competent to give it; also the balance of the curriculum and the atmosphere of the school society should be such as to encourage the development of personality — body, mind and spirit — in due proportions.

(i) Bearing in mind that education is a life-long process, we urge that in every parish opportunities be given through discussion groups or tutorial classes for the teaching and practice of religion so that worship may grow in depth and be made relevant to life. This applies especially to parents and teachers, so that they may be more qualified for teaching the faith in home and school.

(j) Religious teaching should always include instruction about the expansion of the church throughout the world in the last one hundred and fifty years, and some appreciation of the transformation of social life which it has brought about in the countries to which the gospel has been carried in that period.

(k) Particularly we urge that the neglect of the adolescent population should cease. The primary need here is not necessarily to be met by schooling as now understood, though the raising of the school age to sixteen as promised by the President of the Board of Education is greatly to be desired; but the primary need is that young people should be members of a community wider than the family, of such a character that they appreciate their membership of it, and are conscious of responsibility for its honor and welfare.

(l) The church should take its full share in the general development of adult education and should greatly increase its own activities in adult religious education.

(m)   If the church is to take the part which we desire in stimulating the Christian social conscience, it is essential that the clergy should be recruited and equipped so as to provide effective leadership in the field.   Their training should give them a conviction that Christianity has a message for society as well as individuals.   We commend the consideration of this matter to the commission on the training of the clergy.

All these matters should be the concern of the whole Christian community.   We urge that all Christians unite in the furtherance of these aims. This united action is one way toward that full union without which the church cannot effectively witness to the supremacy of the One God or to true community among men.

Life and Worship

At the heart of all the life and witness of the church is its worship.   This must be so directed and conducted that its relevance to life and to men's actual needs is evident.   For this purpose our traditional forms of Matins and Evensong, presupposing as they do acceptance of the tradition of the church and unfailing regularity of use, are largely unsuitable.   They must in most places be supplemented by services of another type, whether liturgical or not, designed to bring before uninstructed people the truth concerning God as Creator, Redeemer and Sanctifier, his claim upon our lives, our need of his grace and our hope in his love and power.

The Eucharist is to be appreciated as the offering of ourselves and all we are — for the bread and wine are the product of man's labor expended upon the gifts of God — in order that Christ may present us with himself in his perfect self-offering, and that we may receive again from him the very gifts which we have offered, now charged with the divine power, to be shared by us in perfect fellowship; so in our worship we express the ideal of our common life and receive strength to make it more real.

The Good News

The message of the church to those who have faith in God and put that faith into practice is Good News.   Man cannot save himself or his society; but " God hath visited and redeemed his people " and is ready, if they are willing, to lead them " into the way of peace."

Signed on behalf of the Conference —

January 10, 1941   WILLIAM EBOR:

APPENDIX III

A MESSAGE FROM THE NATIONAL STUDY CONFER-
ENCE ON THE CHURCHES AND A JUST AND
DURABLE PEACE

(Delaware, March 1942)

I. GUIDING PRINCIPLES

1. We believe that moral law, no less than physical law, undergirds our world. There is a moral order which is fundamental and eternal, and which is relevant to the corporate life of men and the ordering of human society. If mankind is to escape chaos and recurrent war, social and political institutions must be brought into conformity with this moral order.

2. We believe that the sickness and suffering which afflict our present society are proof of indifference to, as well as direct violation of, the moral law. All share in responsibility for the present evils. There is none who does not need forgiveness. A mood of genuine penitence is therefore demanded of us — individuals and nations alike.

3. We believe that it is contrary to the moral order that nations in their dealings with one another should be motivated by a spirit of revenge and retaliation. Such attitudes will lead, as they always have led, to renewed conflict.

4. We believe that the principle of cooperation and mutual concern, implicit in the moral order and essential to a just and durable peace, calls for a true community of nations. The interdependent life of nations must be ordered by agencies having the duty and the power to promote and safeguard the general welfare of all peoples. Only thus can wrongs be righted and justice and security be achieved. A world of irresponsible, competing and unrestrained national sovereignties, whether acting alone or in alliance or in coalition, is a world of international anarchy. It must make place for a higher and more inclusive authority.

5. We believe that economic security is no less essential than political security to a just and durable peace. Such security nationally and internationally involves among other things the use of material resources and the tools of production to raise the general standard of living. Nations are not economically self-sufficient, and the natural wealth of the world is not evenly distributed. Accordingly the possession of such natural resources should not be looked upon as an opportunity to promote national advantage or to enhance the prosperity of some at the expense of others. Rather such possession is a trust to be discharged in the general interest. This calls for more than an offer to sell to all on equal terms. Such an offer may be a futile gesture unless those in need can, through the selling of their own goods and services, acquire the means of buying. The solution of this prob-

lem, doubtless involving some international organization, must be accepted as a responsibility by those who possess natural resources needed by others.

6. We believe that international machinery is required to facilitate the easing of such economic and political tensions as are inevitably recurrent in a world which is living and therefore changing. Any attempt to freeze an order of society by inflexible treaty specifications is bound, in the long run, to jeopardize the peace of mankind. Nor must it be forgotten that refusal to assent to needed change may be as immoral as the attempt by violent means to force such change.

7. We believe that that government which derives its just powers from the consent of the governed is the truest expression of the rights and dignity of man. This requires that we seek autonomy for all subject and colonial peoples. Until that shall be realized, the task of colonial government is no longer one of exclusive national concern. It must be recognized as a common responsibility of mankind, to be carried out in the interests of the colonial peoples by the most appropriate form of organization. This would, in many cases, make colonial government a task of international collaboration for the benefit of colonial peoples who would, themselves, have a voice in their government. As the agencies for the promotion of worldwide political and economic security become effective, the moral, social and material welfare of colonial populations can be more fully realized.

8. We believe that military establishments should be internationally controlled and be made subject to law under the community of nations. For one or more nations to be forcibly deprived of their arms while other nations retain the right of maintaining or expanding their military establishments can only produce an uneasy peace for a limited period. Any initial arrangement which falls short of this must therefore be looked upon as temporary and provisional.

9. We believe that the right of all men to pursue work of their own choosing and to enjoy security from want and oppression is not limited by race, color or creed. The rights and liberties of racial and religious minorities in all lands should be recognized and safeguarded. Freedom of religious worship, of speech and assembly, of the press, and of scientific inquiry and teaching are fundamental to human development and in keeping with the moral order.

10. We believe that, in bringing international relations into conformity with the moral law, a very heavy responsibility devolves upon the United States. For at least a generation we have held preponderant economic power in the world, and with it the capacity to influence decisively the shaping of world events. It should be a matter of shame and humiliation to us that actually the influences shaping the world have largely been irresponsible forces. Our own positive influence has been impaired because of concentration on self and on our short-range material gains. Many of the major preconditions of a just and durable peace require changes of national

policy on the part of the United States. Among such may be mentioned: equal access to natural resources, economic collaboration, equitable treatment of racial minorities, international control of tariffs, limitation of armaments, participation in world government. We must be ready to subordinate immediate and particular national interests to the welfare of all. If the future is to be other than a repetition of the past, the United States must accept the responsibility for constructive action commensurate with its power and opportunity.

11. We believe that a supreme responsibility rests with the church. The church, being a creation of God in Jesus Christ, is called to proclaim to all men everywhere the way of life. Moreover, the church which is now in reality a world community, may be used of God to develop his spirit of righteousness and love in every race and nation and thus to make possible a just and durable peace. For this service Christians must now dedicate themselves, seeking forgiveness for their sins and the constant guidance and help of God.

12. We believe that, as Christian citizens, we must seek to translate our beliefs into practical realities and to create a public opinion which will insure that the United States shall play its full and essential part in the creation of a moral way of international living. We must strive within the life of our own nation for change which will result in the more adequate application here of the principles above enumerated as the basis for a just and durable world order.

13. We believe that the eternal God revealed in Christ is the Ruler of men and of nations and that his purpose in history will be realized. For us he is the source of moral law and the power to make it effective. Amid the darkness and tragedy of the world of today we are upheld by faith that the kingdoms of this world will become the Kingdom of Christ and that he shall reign forever and ever.

II. THE RELATION OF THE CHURCH TO A JUST AND DURABLE PEACE

1. We believe it is the purpose of God to create a world-wide community in Jesus Christ, transcending nation, race and class. The Christian church, accordingly, is responsible not only to proclaim the divine message, but also to contribute by all the means in its power, to secure a world order in which God shall have his rightful place, and the basic needs of mankind shall be satisfied. In the present crisis this responsibility of the church is made more manifest than ever before. It therefore becomes its inescapable duty to speak both to its own members and to the leaders of our political, economic and cultural life concerning what seems to it to be the will of God for the peaceful ordering of human life.

In order that its witness may be effective in the fullest measure, it is important that the church reflect in every phase of its own life — congregational, denominational, interdenominational and ecumenical – the reality of the peace, unity and cooperation which it recommends to secular society.

Conscious also of its helplessness apart from God, and of the infinite resources which it has in God for the supply of every need, the church is called upon to a new ministry of prayer in order that God's saving power may become manifest amid the complexity and tragedy of our life.

2. We are penitently conscious of the many weaknesses and shortcomings of the church itself in the face of the tremendous responsibilities with which it is confronted. We have not sufficiently borne witness to, nor even adequately recognized for the church itself, that very unity of mankind, beyond race and nation, which again and again we have declared in principle.

We call upon our churches, therefore, to enter seriously and immediately upon the task of breaking down the barriers that so easily divide us into opposing groups. We would say to them: If you believe in peace for the world, if you are working for cooperation between nations, governments, races and peoples under the fatherhood of God, you must set the example for such reconciliation and cooperation. The Christian churches must come to realize as they now do not, that joining the Church of Christ in any of its branches means entering a fellowship world-wide in extent, beyond denomination and race, and should involve responsible participation in the task of making spiritually more real our mystical fellowship in community life and in the world.

We would also call upon our churches to enter upon a new era of interdenominational cooperation in which the claims of cooperative effort should be placed, so far as possible, before denominational prestige, and that conjoint Christian efforts be not weakened or imperiled by our several denominational allegiances.

3. We declare as the major premise that the church is a spiritual entity, one and indivisible, which as such is not and cannot be broken by human conflicts. Therefore the church is in a unique position to heal the wounds of war and bind the world together in a just and durable peace. We recognize the particular rights and responsibilities of the state in connection with the secular order. But we reaffirm the Christian truth that the church in its essential nature is an ecumenical, supranational body, separate from and independent of all states including our own national state. The spiritual responsibilities of the church and the spiritual service which it may render derive not from the claims which the state may make but from the freedom and autonomy of the church itself under the Lord Jesus Christ who is its living Head.

4. We believe that each local church will do much to create the mood out of which a just and durable peace can grow, and make its own message of Christian brotherhood real to itself and its constituency, if it will give itself to specific acts of service and reconciliation within its own community.

The practice of acts of interracial good will, aid and friendship for new

Americans, assistance to refugees and to bewildered but innocent aliens, a ministry to the victims of war at home and abroad — these and other such immediate acts of helpfulness will be the best educational experience for the church group itself and will build the community attitudes upon which the peace we seek may later come.

[Various proposals "to prepare and administer an inclusive educational program designed to promote a just and durable peace" were outlined at this point.]

Moreover, in order effectively to convey to governmental authorities the mind of the church on principles pertaining to a just and durable peace, we recommend to the Commission on the Bases of a Just and Durable Peace

(a) That studies be undertaken to ascertain: opinions among church members about social justice and peace; areas where information is lacking; methods of meeting needs thus revealed; best techniques of peace education and action by local churches; ways in which ideals of Christian citizens may be brought into relation with the attitudes of legislative authorities.

(b) That the church be kept informed about legislative proposals and actions, and be aided in rightly understanding their significance.

(c) That full and understanding support be given the efforts of government officials who are promoting farsighted peace proposals.

(d) That churches be informed of the present work of the World Council of Churches, now in process of formation, in steps preliminary to a just peace and that their active cooperation be solicited.

(e) That preparation for a session of the World Council be encouraged in order that through such a session the influence of Christian thought be brought to bear upon the formulation of plans for peace settlement, and that arrangements be made for an adequate Christian representation to meet whenever and wherever any official peace conference or conferences may be held.

5. We believe that if the churches of America are to participate adequately in making peace just and durable, they must develop a more real and vital sense of mission to mankind in the name of Christ, recognizing responsibility for service to humanity in all areas of life, social as well as geographical.

The finest expression of that sense of mission is to be found, we believe, in the missionary enterprises of the church world-wide. However, the aftermath of war on a world scale will necessitate widespread readjustment of program and service to meet the tremendous need of the world. We recommend, therefore:

(a) That the mission boards through cooperative agencies should, at the earliest possible moment, be prepared to interpret to the churches the new opportunities and the necessary adjustments of machinery and study, whatever drastic changes such adjustments may involve.

(b) That a call be issued, if possible through the World Council of Churches, for a more thoroughgoing participation in the world mission of the church, urging at the same time close and warmer cooperation among Christians of *all* lands, in working together in Christ's name for our brothermen everywhere.

III. THE POLITICAL BASES OF A JUST AND DURABLE PEACE

The churches of America face clear responsibilities in seeking to establish a better world when the war has ended. First among postwar duties will be the achievement of a just peace settlement with due regard to the welfare of all nations, the vanquished, the overrun and the victors alike.

In order that such a settlement may tend toward a better political order, we as citizens of the United States of America advocate the following principles and measures:

1. That the United States pursue a responsible national policy with concern for the welfare of all peoples and that the United States cooperate fully with all nations and peoples in working towards a world order of justice and peace.

2. That during a transitional period after the fighting has ended, the efforts of the peoples of the world be devoted, in proportion to their ability, to the re-establishment of order, the provision of food, shelter and medical service, and the restoration of stable government and economic activity, especially in the devastated territories. These emergency measures must include policing by joint action for the protection of minorities and disarmed populations, and positive measures of economic and cultural cooperation. They should be carried out under international authorities, representative of all peoples concerned. There should be no punitive reparations, no humiliating decrees of war guilt, and no arbitrary dismemberment of nations. All of these emergency measures should tend toward a growing structure of international order.

3. That among the functions of government that must be performed are the preservation of public order, the maintenance of economic opportunity, the safeguarding of public health and welfare, and the direction of population movements. In large part, these functions must be performed by local and national governments, but in part they can now be effectively carried out only by international authority.

4. That certain powers now exercised by national governments must, therefore, be delegated to international government, organized and acting in accordance with a world system of law. Among the powers so delegated must be the power of final judgment in controversies between nations, the maintenance and use of armed forces except for preservation of domestic order, and the regulation of international trade and population movements among nations.

5. That international authorities competent to perform these functions may be of two sorts. (1) The ultimate requirement is a duly constituted world government of delegated powers: an international legislative body,

an international court with adequate jurisdiction, international administrative bodies with necessary powers, and adequate international police forces and provision for world-wide economic sanctions. (2) As steps toward, and potential organs of, such world government, there is need for many sorts of international bodies charged with specific duties, such as the International Labor Organization, and various agencies such as those now acting for the United Nations to coordinate natural resources, shipping and food distribution. Such bodies must be adapted to the service of world order and government, and must not become a substitute therefor. In the operation of these agencies, and in progressing toward full world government, every effort should be made to achieve agreement and voluntary cooperation of all concerned.

6. That, utilizing experience with the mandate principle, a system of administration of colonial territories under international authority be developed. In areas now under colonial administration, advance toward self-government should be carried forward in substantial progress. The affairs of peoples deemed not yet capable of self-government should be administered as a common trust, by international authority, in the interest of these peoples as members of a world society.

7. That the influence of the churches shall be employed to keep the foregoing principles before the attention of diplomats and statesmen.

IV. THE ECONOMIC BASES OF A JUST AND DURABLE PEACE

1. Our concern with world economics is an obvious consequence of our desire, as Christians, to realize an ever richer spiritual world fellowship. While the strengthening of the spiritual bond may help to prepare for a solution of the economic problems of the world, the spiritual union may itself be gravely impaired or disrupted by conflict arising in the economic realm. We are deeply disturbed by the economic distress of millions of our fellow men and by economic conditions that threaten the extension of the Kingdom of God on earth.

2. We view the economic tensions and distresses of our day as symptoms of a general world disorder. In our era production has been carried on primarily with a view to monetary gains. Profit has been the principal incentive relied upon to turn the wheels of industry and to bring forth the fruits of the soil.

This system has in recent years developed grave defects. There have occurred mass unemployment, widespread dispossession from homes and farms, destitution, lack of opportunity for youth and of security for old age. These calamities, which have often been accentuated by short-range, self-seeking trade policies of various nations, have made for war. There has been a sharp increase in economic nationalism, with tariffs being raised, monetary systems adjusted for the benefit of national interests, and a race for colonies on the part of some countries. Out of this economic insecurity has come an atmosphere favorable to the rise of demagogues and dictators. Mass unrest has afforded violent and unscrupulous men the opportunity to seize leadership and has made any rational approach to international disputes impossible.

In this chaotic situation there has arisen in certain countries an alternative way of production which is based on complete management and control of all economic life by government. With this has come a system of compulsion which deprives the individual of freedoms, economic, intellectual and spiritual, necessary to human dignity.

We do not believe that we are limited to a choice between these two alternatives. If this seems the only choice it is largely because the churches have failed generally to inculcate Christian motivation. Willingness to strive and to produce and to render services should not be dependent either wholly upon profit motivation or wholly upon compulsion. We urge upon the churches that they have the great opportunity and responsibility to make possible a generally acceptable solution by bringing people to a different and more Christian motivation.

In a day when revolutionary upheavals have swept away the traditional economic organization in Russia, Italy and Germany, and now when, by reason of the necessities of war, that economic order is being radically reorganized everywhere, the church has a manifest duty in the economic field, both urban and rural. That duty is not to line up on the side of any economic system and certainly not to prescribe details or advocate panaceas. Its responsibility lies in a deeper moral realm. As Christians we must be vitally concerned for the preservation of human values in any and every system. The Christian doctrine of man as a child of God carries with it the demand that all men, without distinction of race, creed or class, shall be afforded the economic means of life and growth.

Any economic program which allows the quest for private gain to disregard human welfare, which regiments human beings and denies them freedom of collective bargaining, thus reducing labor to a mere commodity; any program which results in mass unemployment or dire poverty in mine or factory or farm; any program which fails to conserve natural resources and results in soil deterioration and erosion and along with it human erosion and deterioration of rural life in home and school and church, is manifestly wrong. Against such evils the church should arouse the conscience of mankind in every nation. The church must demand economic arrangements measured by human welfare as revealed by secure employment, decent homes and living conditions, opportunity for youth, freedom of occupation and of cultural activities, recognition of the rights of labor, and security in illness and old age. To secure these arrangements it must appeal to the Christian motive of human service as paramount to personal or governmental coercion.

3. The building of a just and peaceful world involves the building of national and local communities on the basis of justice, freedom and cooperation for the common good.

We believe that a new ordering of economic life is both imminent and imperative, and that it will come either through voluntary cooperation within the framework of democracy or through explosive political revolution. We recognize the need of experimentation with various forms of ownership and control, private, cooperative and public. It is hardly to be supposed that any one system, whether of private, cooperative or public enterprise, is suited to all kinds of production, distribution and service. The production and distribution of goods on the basis of voluntary cooperation is an experiment which in many parts of the world is meeting with notable success.

4. We believe that no nation or group of nations can solve in a permanent way the economic problems interior to itself without the cooperation in good will of the other peoples of the world. The economic prosperity of one nation bears a direct and not an inverse ratio to that of others. It is necessary to abandon injurious forms of economic competition and to avoid entrance upon the disastrous chain of economic countermeasures and reprisals which often mark the policy of competing nations. We endorse the principle that "national interdependence now replaces independence and that action by any nation, notably in the economic field, which materially and adversely affects other people, is not purely a matter of domestic policy but is coupled with an international responsibility."

Recommendations Based on Paragraph 3

1. That every man should have the opportunity to share in the ownership of both personal and productive property, such as a home, a farm and economic enterprises.

2. That every member and family of the human race have a right to steady employment and to earn an income such as may provide the necessities of life and growth and is in accord with the wealth-producing capacity of their day and the requirements of responsible conservation of natural resources.

3. That in early years every individual has the right to full-time educational opportunities with reasonable consideration of his talents, interests and probable vocation; that in later years every individual is entitled to economic security in retirement and the continuation of cultural opportunities; that in the whole span of life every individual is entitled to adequate health service and professional medical care; and that in the productive years there is the universal obligation to work in some socially necessary service.

4. That every man has the right to employment of a kind that is consistent with human dignity and self-respect, and to such leisure as is essential for cultural and spiritual development; that employers of all kinds should recognize and safeguard these rights.

5. That citizens, through their governments or other appropriate agencies, have not only the right but the duty

(a) To prevent destructive cyclical trends in business by regulatory measures or, if these prove inadequate, by direct initiative;

(b) To counteract the unemployment resulting from technological change through vocational re-education, through public employment agencies and, if necessary, through a reorganization of industries and markets.

6. That industrial democracy is fundamental to successful political democracy, and we therefore recommend that labor be given an increasing responsibility for and participation in industrial management. The principle of democracy in economic relations should be accorded wider expression by the development of stronger *voluntary* producers associations, farm organizations, labor organizations, professional groups, and consumers organizations, and their integration into some form of national economic council, for planning in cooperation with government for maximum production and consumption and the abolition of unemployment. In each industry also, industrial councils should be developed, representative of management, labor and consumers, for democratic direction of industries toward these same ends. The effect of maximum production and consumption in each country would be to decrease the pressure of competition for world markets and thus to mitigate one of the major economic causes of war.

7. That we cannot find the means of preventing social disorder until we have ended the paradox of poverty in the midst of plenty. We believe that a tax program should be formulated in such a way that the burden be placed in proportion to the ability to pay, to the end that our wealth may be more equitably distributed.

8. That agriculture has a dual importance, both as a way of making a living and as a basis of family and community life. Our economic system must become servant and not master in maintaining the socially significant services of agriculture, such as feeding the world and producing the organic raw materials essential to industry.

9. In view of the Christian principle that a house divided against itself cannot stand, we urge that the International Labor Organization or its successor organization after the war shall make a special study of all available plans for avoiding or reducing the animosities too often prevailing between labor and management and tending to national inefficiency and war.

Recommendations Based on Paragraph 4

1. The progressive elimination of restrictions on world trade, such as tariffs and quotas, under the guidance of an international organization and by other appropriate methods.

2. "The fullest collaboration between all nations in the economic field with the object of securing *for all* improved labor standards, economic advancement and social security." This is the language of the Atlantic Charter, Article 5. We call attention however to the fact that in Article 4 of this charter, the obligation "to further the enjoyment by all states, great or small, victor or vanquished, of access on equal terms to the trade and raw materials of the world which are needed for their economic prosperity," is limited by the phrase, "with due respect for their existing obligations." We urge that such existing obligations be modified so as to permit the complete

achievement of the goal set forth in this same article. We hold that in all this matter the rights and needs of indigenous populations should be given just consideration.

3. The establishment of a universal system of money. The money system should be so planned as to prevent inflation and deflation, in so far as this is possible through monetary means.

4. The establishment of a democratically controlled international bank or banks to make development capital available in all parts of the world without the predatory or imperialistic aftermath so characteristic of large-scale private or governmental loans.

5. The creation of a world organization to study and make recommendations concerning problems arising from the pressure of population on the means of subsistence. We condemn any attempt upon the part of any nation to solve these problems by measures that discriminate against any people because of race or creed.

We believe that wealthy nations should not only refrain from action that is injurious to their neighbors, but should initiate action that is calculated to benefit their neighbors, as for example the direction of foreign investments with a view to raising the standard of living of the underprivileged peoples of the earth. No attempt should be made, however, to *impose* an alien culture upon any people.

We recognize that at the close of the war vast populations will be in need of food, shelter, clothing and medical care, and that vast areas will call for physical and economic rehabilitation. We believe that the American people, acting through their government, should assume a major share of the responsibility and task of meeting this need.

General Resolution on Economic Collaboration

We note such acts of our government as that reported by Undersecretary of State Welles at Rio de Janeiro on January 15, 1942, that "It is the policy of the United States to aid in maintaining the economic stability of the other American republics by recognizing and providing for their essential civilian needs on the basis of equal and proportionate consideration with our own"; also the provisions of Article 7 of the Anglo-American Pact of February 26, 1942, calling for "postwar participation, by all countries of like mind, directed to the expansion, by appropriate international and domestic measures, of production, employment and exchanging consumption of goods which are the material foundations of the liberty and welfare of all peoples; to the elimination of all forms of discriminatory treatment in international commerce, and to the reduction of tariffs and other trade barriers." We instruct the officers of this conference to communicate to our government our deep satisfaction with such acts. The spirit evidenced thereby is, in our judgment, that which must come to permeate the life of nations if they are to achieve a just and durable peace.

V. THE SOCIAL BASES OF A JUST AND DURABLE PEACE
Principles

We are convinced that the present struggle of the nations is not just another war in the history of mankind. It is the upheaval of the old order and the birth of a new. The relationships of men will never again be the same, nor should they be the same, for they have not been founded on the eternal truths of God.

Therefore we affirm that whatever peace settlements are presented to the peoples of the world should express the following principles:

1. Man is a child of God and all men are brothers one of another. The church in its long-established missionary work recognizes its responsibility to bring all men into full relationship as children of God.

2. Mankind is one in nature and in the sight of God. No group of men is inherently superior or inferior to any other, and none is above any other beloved of God.

3. The whole earth is given by God and to all men for their common dwelling place, and the resources of the earth should be used as his gifts to the whole human family.

4. All men should be free to move over the surface of the earth under international agreement, in search of the fullest opportunity for personal development.

5. Freedom of religious worship, of speech and assembly, of conscience, of the press, of the arts, and of scientific inquiry and teaching should be available to all men everywhere.

Relief and Rehabilitation

The present mass suffering of the world requires action on the part of the church in America far beyond anything yet undertaken. Six million young men in the prison camps of the world; scores of millions of refugees — homeless, helpless, starving; whole regions subjected to slow starvation as a result of the policies of states — these and kindred areas of desperate suffering inflicted upon masses of innocent victims challenge the church to a demonstration of its basic doctrines of human solidarity and brotherhood in a potential family of God. They provide potent opportunities for creating even now, in the midst of war, responses of good will and solid grounds for enduring fellowship.

Toward a World Community

The nations of the world are passing through the crucible of fire and sword. National cultures which have enriched and given meaning to millions of people are in danger of extinction. No nation can escape this crisis. Those nations which, amid the purifying days of suffering, rediscover or preserve their souls from disintegration under the heel of the invader, from the despair of defeat, or from the pride and boastfulness of victory, will be ready to reconstruct their own national life and that of the world upon the ruins of today.

The sovereign power of the nation-state is being modified by economic, political and military forces which demand a new social order. It will be impossible to return to such extreme practices of national sovereignty as have prevailed during recent decades. We believe that the state is a form of political organization which can and should be modified to meet the needs of the peoples of the world in the emerging situation. At the same time, however, we believe that different peoples have their distinctive places in the divine economy and that any world order must look toward unity in diversity and not to general internationalism and cosmopolitanism. If we would avoid a superficial solution to the world's needs, we must come to recognize the distinction between those cultural values that center around the people, or folk, on the one hand, and the political state and government on the other.

We, the members of the American churches and a part of the world-wide Christian community, believe that the Christian churches in those countries where they are an inherent part of its nation's life, have a task to perform not only in helping to preserve and restore the national spiritual unity of their people but also in relating their people to the larger family of nations.

We believe that no matter what world scheme for political and economic organization may be devised to meet the demands of the modern world, at the heart of such a plan there must be developed an "international ethos" which not only springs from the loyalties of the people to their own nation, but includes their relationship to the welfare of mankind as a whole.

We believe that the Christian church, because of its universal gospel, its positive world view and its deep concern for both the individual and the nation, stands on the threshold of its greatest opportunity to bear witness to the reality of the world Christian community and to manifest in sacrificial living a spirit through which a suffering, broken humanity can be transformed into a world community.

Race Relations and Cultures

Among the primary factors in the maintenance of a just and durable peace will be equitable treatment of all racial groups that make up the world's population. Therefore the securing of justice now for racial groups is essential if America is to make its full contribution in securing a just and durable peace.

We acknowledge with profound contrition the sin of racial discrimination in American life and our own share, though we are Christians, in the common guilt. So long as our attitudes and policies deny peoples of other races in our own or other lands the essential position of brothers in the common family of mankind we cannot safely be trusted with the making of a just and durable peace.

In our own country millions of people, especially American Negroes, are subjected to discrimination and unequal treatment in educational opportunities, in employment, wages and conditions of work, in access to professional and business opportunities, in housing, in transportation, in the administration of justice and even in the right to vote. We condemn all such inequalities and call upon our fellow Christians and fellow citizens to initiate and support measures to establish equality of status and treatment of members of minority racial and cultural groups.

Some local current outrages that have national significance and therefore international effects in the attitudes of other peoples are the recent Missouri lynching and the rioting in Detroit over the Sojourner Truth Housing Project.

The conference adopted the following:

A. Under *Relief and Rehabilitation*

To rise adequately to a sense of its God-given mission, the church must:

1. Make vivid in the consciousness of its entire membership the awful reality of this agony — mass in extent, but personal in intensity.

2. Provide continual opportunity for material giving on the part of every member, to the point of genuine sacrifice, as a requisite of Christian living.

3. Recognize cooperating agencies approved by the Committee on Foreign Relief Appeals in the Churches as existing channels for a world-wide ministry of compassion: (1) War Prisoners' Aid of the World's Committee of the Y.M.C.A.; (2) Central Bureau for Relief of the Evangelical Churches of Europe; (3) Church Committee for China Relief; (4) American Bible Society; (5) American Friends Service Committee; (6) Y.W.C.A. World Emergency Fund; (7) American Committee for Christian Refugees; (8) International Missionary Council.

4. Recognize responsibilities for cooperation with government in areas of rehabilitation which concern the church but transcend its normal functions. Such areas include the moving of populations, the restoration of the cultural life of peoples, the resettling of refugees, the return and rehabilitation of prisoners of war, and the reintegration into civilian life of men in the armed forces and the Civilian Public Service camps.

The malnutrition and slow starvation of millions of innocent victims of war in conquered countries is heavy upon our Christian consciences. Although we have not reached agreement as to immediate remedial measures to be urged upon governments, we request the Federal Council of Churches to continue its exploration with the governmental authorities with a view to finding practicable means for alleviating these situations.

5. Prepare now for the tasks of rehabilitation at the end of the war. Such preparation might well include the following:

(a) Relate present war relief giving to the continuing need which the end of the war will not terminate but only more clearly reveal.

(b) Develop courses and emphases in church schools and young people's programs regarding the problems of reconstruction which will prepare our youth for their responsibility. Specialized training should be provided for those people who may be called to serve in reconstruction abroad.

(c) Urge missionary societies to maintain intact, so far as is possible, their field organizations and personnel for large-scale and effective reconstruction.

(d) Ask missionary agencies to emphasize a thorough grounding in the technique of relief and rehabilitation for all candidates in training for missionary service.

B. Under *Toward a World Community*

We urge among some of the problems for further study by church people the following statements:

1. The highest ethical principles which in their operation have hitherto been limited to community and national relationships should now be so extended as to apply in the field of international relations.

2. The problem confronting the world is how to substitute for the idea of self-preservation of the individual state a concept of world order which will recognize the primary importance of the society of nations, and the principle that the good of the whole takes precedence over the good of the part, since the highest and ultimate good of the part is itself so largely conditioned by the good of the whole.

3. Whatever may be the political, economic or military form of world organization for the preservation of a just and durable peace, the rights and duties of peoples to maintain their full cultural freedom must be preserved.

Many of the Christian churches in the lands of the conquerors and the conquered have during these tragic days remained faithful to the Master. With the central message of the Cross, they have succored the souls of their peoples and have kept them from despair. They have pointed to the God-imposed duty of every people, no matter how small or how large, of whatever race or creed, to go the way of repentance, obedience and complete consecration to his will.

C. Under *Race Relations and Culture*

1. We commend the President of the United States for his executive action directed toward the elimination of discrimination in industry and the public services against Negroes and persons of other racial and national origin. We urge that in further pursuit of this policy Negro Americans be given suitable recognition in the administrative and judicial departments of the government.

2. We call our fellow Christians to witness that it is in the nature of the church that Negro men and women and those belonging to other racial and national minorities should be welcomed into the membership, administrative personnel and fellowship of our churches, local and national. We urge individual Christians and the corporate body of the church of Christ to take

up the cross of courageous service in action which deals with the problems of race and color in our land.

3. The modern confusion of culture and race has grown out of the belief that culture is a product of biological heredity and that Anglo-European culture is superior because it has sprung from superior human strains. We believe that all racial groups have contributed outstanding cultural gifts to civilization and that the exchange of such gifts has enriched all mankind. A just and durable peace should provide and insist upon a framework that allows more opportunity for creative expression of all groups and for greater exchange of such cultural creations in the field of music, art, medicine and literature. Assimilation of culture does not mean amalgamation of racial stocks.

4. We appeal to our fellow citizens to recognize now the crucial importance of justice in race relations in our own country as paving the way for the wider recognition of it which will be essential to world peace. Our attitudes toward other racial groups have all too frequently prevented the operation of justice in the past. We remind our fellow Christians of the appeal of the Japanese for recognition of racial equality at the time of the Versailles peace conference. The refusal of that plea and the imposing of such restrictions on immigration as embodied in the Immigration Act of 1924 are recognized as factors contributing to the breakdown of peace. We would now commit ourselves to the task of protecting the rights of American-born citizens of Oriental parentage, who are likely to suffer unnecessarily because of racial prejudice and discrimination of our attitudes towards Asiatics.

5. We endorse the proposal that the Federal Council of the Churches of Christ in America set up a commission for the study of racial and cultural problems in American life as a necessary measure to support our effort for a just and durable peace among the nations. It is imperative that we put our own house in order so that we can contribute effectively to a sound organization of international life. To that end we need continuous study, interpretation and a device to guide our churches in facing the opportunities and duties of racial and cultural adjustment in the present crisis, both at home and abroad.

6. Also, when further statements of peace aims are made, we ask our government to clarify in more detail its peace aims toward recognizing racial equality, opportunity and aid for migration, and protection of religious, political, racial and cultural minorities.

APPENDIX IV

A STATEMENT OF POLITICAL PROPOSITIONS

(Popularly known as the Six Pillars of Peace)

1. The peace must provide the political framework for a continuing collaboration of the United Nations and, in due course, of neutral and enemy nations.

2. The peace must make provision for bringing within the scope of international agreement those economic and financial acts of national governments which have widespread international repercussions.

3. The peace must make provision for an organization to adapt the treaty structure of the world to changing underlying conditions.

4. The peace must proclaim the goal of autonomy for subject peoples, and it must establish international organization to assure and to supervise the realization of that end.

5. The peace must establish procedures for controlling military establishments everywhere.

6. The peace must establish in principle, and seek to achieve in practice, the right of individuals everywhere to religious and intellectual liberty.

APPENDIX V

A CHRISTIAN MESSAGE ON WORLD ORDER FROM THE INTERNATIONAL ROUND TABLE OF CHRISTIAN LEADERS

(Princeton, July 1943)

I. TO THE WORLD

The Christian church believes and declares to the world that "there is a moral order which is fundamental and eternal," and that "if mankind is to escape chaos and recurrent war, social and political institutions must be brought into conformity with this moral order." (*Guiding Principles*, approved by the National Study Conference at Delaware, Ohio.) This moral order is the will of God, the Creator of mankind. Basic in it are the law of justice and the principle that man should love his neighbor as himself.

The Christian church believes and declares the gospel that God in Christ enables man to overcome his sinful defiance of the moral order. While such defiance persists, those who seek to do his will must strive to restrain the power and effect of evil, and to introduce order into society by extending to human relationships the rule of just and good laws.

Such efforts are urgently needed in relationships between nations. On the basic moral principles of justice and the love of one's neighbor as oneself, the church must call for consideration of:

1. The extent to which each state should accept the establishment of an international authority responsible for the maintenance of law and order among the nations and for limiting the independent national control of armed forces.

2. The extent to which each state should limit the independent ordering of its economic life in such matters as tariffs, import quotas and currency, with a view to promoting the common welfare of mankind.

3. The government of one people by another (as in the case of colonies, or defeated nations) and the degree of international control required to insure that such government, where it exists, shall be used for the purpose of preparing the way for equality.

4. How race prejudice may be overcome, equal dignity and opportunity accorded to all races, and justice secured to religious and racial minorities.

In the consideration of these subjects it is necessary to make judgments on technical matters and questions of human behavior. These judgments, to have any effect, must be crystallized in proposals which, being subject to human fallibility, must be distinguished from the primary principles which carry the authority of the gospel. In concrete situations, action to implement the principles demands that decisions be made involving the adoption of particular proposals.

Concern for world order, then, is for us an imperative obligation inherent in the Christian world view. A weary and frustrated world needs and desires a clear statement of a goal toward which to strive. Therefore there is demanded of us a positive affirmation of our faith and purpose as directed toward the problem of world order. Such an affirmation should arouse a spirit more dynamic than that which impels other movements seeking universal acceptance. Our faith and purpose derive from the conviction that they are in conformity with God's purpose in history and are therefore required by divine mandate. To support us we have the guidance and power of the Holy Spirit.

We are committed to the goal of world-wide political order, and thus to the establishment of the institutions or organizations best suited to serve this end. The need for action is urgent. We recognize, however, that our objective may not be fully attainable at a single step but may have to be evolved through intermediate developments. We are concerned, therefore, both with the goal and with the program of next steps — international conferences and the administration of relief and reconstruction, for example. These next steps must be consonant with the goal; otherwise they may lead away from it.

Principles Fundamental to World Order

Certain principles must be accepted with which both the world-wide organizations for world order and the immediate steps must conform: (1) The imperative of moral law; (2) the worth of every human being; (3) the precedence of human over material values and considerations; (4) the individual's responsibility for collective action taken in his name; (5) the moral duty of cooperative action.

These principles must not be compromised out of considerations of expediency. On the other hand, we realize that no institution can give them full expression.

If the progressively achieved world organization effectively serves the values inherent in these principles and consequently assures national security, it will win the loyalty of nations and will not depend for its support primarily upon treaty obligations or imposed force.

Certain Political Propositions

In order to bring about the initial and vital decision on the direction in which nations will move within the political area, we set forth six political propositions (Six Pillars of Peace) heretofore formulated by the Commission to Study the Bases of a Just and Durable Peace. We welcome these as indicative of what the people of all nations should study, understand and accept in relation to the conditions by which they are confronted; and seek through appropriate channels to have accepted by their governments. (See Appendix IV.)

Requirements for Progress Toward World Order

Progress toward our goal will require:

1. That national isolationism, the monopolization of political power by a few nations, and the balance of power which hitherto have failed to maintain peace, be repudiated as policies which contravene the purpose of establishing world order and the institutions requisite thereto.

2. That temporary collaboration among the United Nations should, as quickly as possible, give way to a universal order and not be consolidated into a closed military alliance to establish a preponderance of power or a concert of power.

3. That drastic reduction in armaments be undertaken as a step toward the goals envisaged in the Atlantic Charter of the "abandonment of the use of force" and lifting from the peoples of the world "the crushing burden of armaments."

4. That immediate international collaboration such as is involved in (a) conferences dealing with specific problems and in (b) the administration of relief and reconstruction be guarded against exploitation for purposes of power politics.

5. That if regional organizations arise, they be part of an inclusive world order and shall not threaten the interests of world organization.

6. That a larger measure of discipline and sacrifice for the good of the whole world community be practiced by each nation as necessary to the good of that nation as a part of the community.

7. That individual citizens recognize their responsibility for their collective decisions as reflected in national policies.

8. That ethical and moral standards recognized as applying to individual conduct be recognized as applying also to group, corporate and national conduct.

9. That cultural and social collaborations be established, along with political collaboration, as essential for the achievement of world order.

10. That an adequate motivation be developed in the will of the peoples of the world to support the agencies and arrangements for cooperation, so that the sense of national destiny which has hitherto led nations to seek national aggrandizement, shall hereafter find its expression in works that promote the general welfare of mankind.

II. TO THE CHURCH

The Christian church itself is potentially the chief instrument of world order. The desperate needs of the people are for moral and spiritual light, for release from fear, for faith and courage, for forgiveness and the grace to forgive. It is the responsibility of the church to meet those needs.

For such a day as this, God has brought to the church a new access of power in unity. The recognition of this fact has brought renewed hope and courage to Christians in all lands. Stockholm, Lausanne, Oxford, Edinburgh, Madras and Amsterdam have become symbols of light in a dark world. Youth especially is being drawn to this new reality and life. The emergence of the World Council of Churches and the increasing vitality of the other ecumenical organizations have occurred at a time when the world has been torn asunder by conflict. Even now, the ecumenical character of the church demonstrates its reality. Across all lines of cleavage the ecumenical fellowship has not only endured but has been maturing. In its ministry to prisoners of war, in the support of stranded missionaries by churches of other nations and denominations, in a study program in many lands, its practical service is being enlarged. It is a church made new, and yet the same church that has spanned the centuries, proclaiming judgment and salvation while civilizations and empires have risen and fallen.

Included within the church's mission are the following responsibilities:

1. The church must lead the world to God through Christ. The opportunity is unprecedented. Disillusionment regarding false leaders and misdirected loyalties to lost causes is creating a spiritual vacuum for many people. A proud generation has already been somewhat subdued by the realization that our own unaided resources are not enough for living in this world. As the people are brought into the peace and power of God and to an acceptance of his will for our human relationships, an adequate faith for living will be formed. Human personality will be rebuilt and the motivation will be developed to make more effective the instruments of world order.

2. The churches in their own life, as members of a world-wide fellowship, must give a demonstration of orderly and mutually helpful community. The basic social problem of world order is that of achieving moral and spiritual community. The ecumenical church, made up of different denominations, with members from all the different races, nations and classes, is called upon to show how the common relationship of its members to Jesus Christ has provided a basis of unity, upon which differences can be harmonized and community achieved. Further, it will require that the churches instruct their ministers and members as to the meaning of the ecumenical church, thus creating the ecumenical mind which will analyze all problems of relations between races, classes and nations from the point of view of the world-wide Christian brotherhood.

The churches in their corporate relationships, wherever they themselves are a part of the world order, and in their programs of evangelism, education and social action, locally, nationally and internationally, should practice in their own life the principles which they recommend to others, and create new patterns and expressions of brotherhood which will be an example to the secular community.

3. The churches in the ecumenical fellowship should seek to achieve common agreement upon the basic moral principles of national and international policy inherent in their common faith. Thus they will contribute to the development of a common ethos, without which political order will be at best unstable. For example, they will challenge and counteract the development of hatred which tends to increase under the tensions and outrages of war, and the development of intolerance of which anti-Semitism has been a flagrant example.

4. The churches must call the nations and governments to moral responsibility under God; for states subsist under the governance of God and are not morally autonomous. This will require that the churches themselves challenge the nations and governments to conform to moral law. It will require also that they educate their members to see the necessity to increase and extend the acceptance of the responsibilities of Christian vocation as citizens. Such vocation demands of the individual (a) that he support and seek to persuade others to support such local and national policies as he believes, on the basis of his enlightened Christian judgment, most closely approximate an application of Christian principles; (b) that he endeavor to elect and support public leaders who are committed to such policies; and (c) that he consider his responsibility to enter service in public office.

For the churches in their corporate life and for the individual members, the profound need of the world for an order of justice, liberty and peace is a sobering but inspiring challenge. For we labor not in dependence upon our own wisdom or strength alone but in confidence in God who ever reigns and who is sufficient to them that are faithful.

" And now unto Him that is able to do exceeding abundantly above all that we ask or think, according to the power that worketh in us, unto Him be glory in the church by Christ Jesus, throughout all ages, world without end. Amen."

SUGGESTED APPLICATIONS OF THE CHRISTIAN MESSAGE IN CERTAIN AREAS

1. Russia

Any planning for world order calls for special consideration of the relationship to such world order of the ideals and practices of the U.S.S.R. The Russian revolution is one of the great facts of our time and its consequences will be central for many years.

In form, and to a large extent in practice, the Russian revolution has been anti-religious and materialistic. If that continues to be the case we cannot disguise our concern. That would prevent a world community of spirit which is an indispensable foundation of world order.

But we need not assume that this will be the case. Unhappily history can show more than one instance where organized religion has seemed an obstacle to needed change, so that revolution to achieve reform has initially tended to assume an anti-clerical character. In the case of the Russian revolution, many of its avowed objectives are those which Christians have long accepted in principle but have largely failed to achieve in practice. Such are the right of all men to work, to rest and leisure, to social security, to education, and to non-discrimination on the basis of race. It was a reflection upon organized Christianity, and that not only in Russia, that the planners of the Russian revolution felt that achievement of such social objectives required the repudiation of Christianity. They were influenced in part by revolutionary doctrine originating elsewhere.

We believe that as Christian people demonstrate that they can achieve such beneficent social ends as are sought by the Russian revolution — and much more besides — many differences between us will tend to disappear. We need not now act on the assumption that those differences will persist to create a permanent barrier to world order.

We realize that in addition to differences of ideas and of philosophy, there are serious and imminent problems involving the territorial relations of the U.S.S.R. to neighboring people. Here again, a just solution does not depend upon Russia alone. A vital objective of Russia, as for the rest of the world, is that of achieving security. Nations that have the power to do so will usually seek strategic boundaries unless satisfied that their security can equally or better be served in some other way, as through a universal order. During the years preceding the outbreak of this war, the U.S.S.R. participated as actively as any other nation in organized efforts to preserve world order and peacefully adjust international differences. We can assume that Russia will still be disposed to participate in any international program that is practical and realistic. Thus what the nations as a whole will now do to create international security will largely determine whether Russia and other great powers will sacrifice to strategic ends the autonomy of distinctive ethnic and cultural groups. The genuine concern of Christian peoples for Russia's neighbors will doubtless appear to Russians to be hypocritical unless their nations are prepared to join in effective steps to create international security.

As a group of Christians outside of Russia we have thought mostly, as we ought, of our own deficiencies in the past and our own peculiar responsibilities for the future. That approach should not, however, be taken as evidence that we have lost confidence in the power of the gospel of Christ or that we acquiesce in the consequence of our past failures. We are profoundly convinced that the Christian interpretation of life and destiny is essential to the realization of human welfare, social justice and world order. Admittedly, organized Christianity has failed to achieve fully these ends. But an anti-Christian or non-Christian society is bound to fail more lamentably. We are also convinced — and this is more important — that the gospel of Christ is needed if individual human beings are to have a proper relationship to God and to their fellow men. That gospel, we are commanded, must be preached in all the world. For all of these reasons we seek in Russia, as elsewhere, conditions of spiritual and intellectual liberty which will make that possible and we eagerly look forward to the day when Christians in Russia may freely and in organized form join with Christian bodies elsewhere in ecumenical fellowship.

2. Germany

(a) A Clash of Ideologies. This war is not merely a conflict of nations; it is a clash of ideologies. Germany is controlled by the demonic forces of racialism and perverted nationalism. These forces are being opposed not only in the free countries of the United Nations and in occupied lands, but also among growing groups in Germany itself. And, it must be admitted, the very same forces find support in some sections of opinion, and even in certain governmental policies, within the United Nations, free and occupied.

Christians are bound to acknowledge with penitence their failures individually and nationally to live up to their professed ideals. This should not hide from them the fact that Nazi ideology avows and embraces monstrous evils as matters of official policy.

In face of this whole situation Christians should beware of thinking solely on nationalistic lines.

(b) Germany within Europe. All Europe has longed for stability and unity. This very aspiration lent Hitler a great measure of his support both within and without Germany. His " new order " has utterly failed. It has, indeed, defeated itself, essentially because its policy was not based upon voluntary cooperation but upon the enforced subordination of Europe to the " master race." Clearly, this policy or any other which seeks its ends by reliance upon division, hatred, bitterness, selfishness and avarice — wherever it may be pursued — is foredoomed.

Any proposal to further European stability, involving 80,000,000 Germans, must be approached with proportionate concern for the problem of the majority of that continent — the 250,000,000 non-Germans, a considerable portion of whom have been deprived of their freedom and means of living.

For the oppressed nations, victims of aggression, justice demands a restitution by Germany, but one that will not involve disintegration of the European economic structure.

For Germany, the aggressor, Christianity involves reconciliation on the basis of justice, and the meeting of a spirit of repentance with a spirit of forgiveness. This attitude must characterize all policies to which Christians lend support.

(c) Germany within World Organization. While the problem of Germany in the postwar period cannot be separated from its European setting, its solution must also take into account the wider objective — the early achievement of world organization embracing all nations. Our object should be to help Germany take her place within this organization, assuming all the responsibilities and rights which membership implies. With regard to the treatment of Germany, Christian principles must prevail. Controls and safeguards will be necessary. But it would be folly to attempt to apply repressive measures so vindictive and harsh that public opinion in the victor nations themselves will later revolt against them. This will inevitably bring about a breakdown of the peace structure and lead to renewed conflict. More powerful than any material forces imposed as safeguards upon Germany will be the invigoration of the sense of personal responsibility on the part of individuals and a world point of view based upon Christian principles influencing and strengthening recuperative forces within Germany.

Churches and nations must lend responsible leaders in Germany every encouragement and aid in the process of creating that Christian world viewpoint, while at the same time demonstrating their sincerity of purpose by initiating whatever re-education is needed in their own sphere of responsibility within their own lands.

(d) Postwar Policy of the United Nations. Guiding principles for the postwar policy of the United Nations have already been laid down in official statements, for example, in the Atlantic Charter. There is a remarkable degree of agreement at many points between these and those proposed by our churches. Christians are concerned to see to it that their respective governments place the highest interpretation upon these principles and that the economic and political policies to be formulated do in fact implement them.

(e) The Churches of Germany in the Postwar World. In seeking to establish order and stability in Germany, the United Nations and their governments in initiating any program aimed at help in the re-establishment of order and stability in Germany will do well to recognize the great assistance which the German churches can give. Among the cultural organizations of Germany, the churches have conspicuously succeeded in retaining their inner coherence, their sense of continuity and their corporate purposes. They have won a deepened loyalty of their people. Mindful of the wealth of spiritual experience which the persecution and consequent resistance of the churches of Germany have produced, we anticipate the contributions which they can make to the whole Christian church. They will be spiritual allies in the realization of common goals.

(f) Ecumenical Christian Fellowship. The essence of the ecumenical church is one Christian fellowship, unbroken by space or circumstance. We welcome with gratitude the certain knowledge, based on authentic evidence, that the sense of spiritual kinship has not been lost by our brethren in the German churches as we are certain it has not been lost by us. In the expression of this ecumenical spirit, we see what Archbishop Temple of Canterbury, head of the Provisional Committee of the World Council of Churches, called " the great new fact of our time . . . one ground of hope for the future."

3. The Far East

Although the terms exacted from Japan will be severe, as Christians, we urge that they be just, constructive, and not retributive. They must not be carried to the point where Japan would be deprived of hope or prospect of economic revival and of readmission into international society with its consequent rights and duties.

Because the restoration of territories now occupied by Japan, notably Formosa, Korea and Manchuria, will inevitably deprive her of important features of the economy which she had built up before the war, steps must be taken (e.g., by providing access to markets for her exports and thus the means of obtaining foodstuffs and other vital materials, and by lending capital) to enable her to adjust her postwar economy to the legitimate welfare of her people without detriment to the economies of her neighbors.

In general, it will be neither possible nor desirable for the victorious powers to impose upon Japan conditions as to her future form of government; but they should shape their policy toward Japan so as to encourage the emergence within Japan of liberal and moderate elements disposed to cooperate in international arrangements for security, and other international projects of a global nature.

While it may be expedient to deal with certain political or economic problems of the Far East by regional machinery, this can be done only within the framework of a global organization of peace and international economic life. The interests and obligations of Occidental countries cannot be isolated from those of Oriental countries. Security above all is a matter of global concern.

Relations between Occidental and Oriental peoples cannot be successfully conducted except upon a basis of the universal nature of human rights and without racial discrimination.

There must be a constructive program for the further development of colonial areas in southeastern Asia, in their own interests and in the interests of the world at large. It must provide for the security and welfare of the indigenous populations, and for an increasing share by them in the government of the countries which they inhabit, with self-government as a goal. Some method should be devised for the exercise of international responsibility for the execution of this program.

A MESSAGE TO THE MANY CHRISTIANS IN WAR-TORN LANDS

A Message to the many Christians separated from us by the barriers of war who remain steadfast in the Faith:

We who address you are a group of Christian men and women who have come together from fourteen lands. We have met to rededicate ourselves to the task of seeking that out of this war will come a just and durable peace. Throughout our proceedings, thought of you has been constantly in our minds.

We want you to know of our deep sense of obligation to you. Despite long years of attempted suppression and oftentimes of persecution, your faith in God as revealed by Jesus Christ has not weakened. Indeed, it has grown stronger until it is now a flaming symbol that all men see. The Christian faith elsewhere has been inspired and nourished by your example.

You have taught us to see better the true meaning of life and what it is that is worth striving for and, if need be, dying for. You have shown us the practice of human fellowship. We are made ashamed that we have done so little where you have risked so much. We have pledged ourselves to new efforts to prevent intolerance anywhere and to secure recognition of the essential dignity of human beings everywhere, without regard for nation, race or creed.

We long to come to you in person and to bring you some material succor and to receive from you the fuller stimulus of your spiritual vigor. We hope and believe that the time for that is not far distant. We know that there must still be much agony of body and soul. But the end is in sight.

When that end comes we hope that the power of the nations will thereafter be made the servant of righteous government and of world order. To assure that will be a task of the Christian forces. We do not minimize the difficulties which confront us. But the vigor of our component parts is now such that we can work mightily once we can again work in unison and freely reinforce one another. More and more is the world receptive, recognizing that moral force provides a basic foundation upon which justice and order can be re-established where all else has been swept away. May the Lord God strengthen your faith and our faith, that we may better serve his holy purpose.

A DECLARATION ON WORLD PEACE

Made by American Protestant, Catholic and Jewish Leaders
(October 6, 1943)

One hundred and forty-four clerical and lay leaders of the Protestant, Catholic and Jewish faiths in the United States on October 6, 1943, made public a joint declaration on basic principles of peace for the postwar world, which were published by the Federal Council of Churches, the National Catholic Welfare Conference and the Synagogue Council of America. This document, although issued too late for discussion in the body of this book, further defines the position of the American churches and synagogues on the issues discussed herein. The full text of the declaration, together with the separate introductions prepared for each of the three faiths, follows.

Protestant

In a world troubled to despair by recurring war the Protestant churches have been seeking to show how moral and religious convictions should guide the relations of nations. Their conclusions are in many important respects similar to those of men of other faiths. In this we rejoice, for world order cannot be achieved without the cooperation of all men of good will. We appeal to our constituency to give heed to the following proposals enunciated by Protestants, Catholics and Jews, which must find expression in national policies. Beyond these proposals we hold that the ultimate foundations of peace require spiritual regeneration as emphasized in the Christian gospel.

Catholic

We present for the consideration of all men of good will the following postulates of a just peace as embodying the principles of the moral law and their prime applications to world problems of our day. To our mind they express the minimum requirements of a peace which Christians can endorse as fair to all men. They are the foundation on which Catholics in a free world can work from deep motives of Christian justice and charity for the building of a better social order.

Jewish

The American synagogue commends to the attention of its own constituency and to all men of faith the following principles as a guide to thought and action in dealing with the grave world problems of our time. These seven principles, while they do not exhaust the teachings of the Jewish tradition on issues of social relationships, have their sanction in Judaism both biblical and rabbinic. Judaism's highest goal has ever been "to amend the world through the Kingdom of God." The synagogue therefore calls upon its adherents, both as citizens and as Jews, to seek after the implementation of these principles. They will thereby act in faithful conformity with the moral values of the Jewish religion, and at the same time serve the best interests of country and of mankind.

The Declaration

1. The organization of a just peace depends upon practical recognition of the fact that not only individuals but nations, states and international society are subject to the sovereignty of God and to the moral law which comes from God.

2. The dignity of the human person as the image of God must be set forth in all its essential implications in an international declaration of rights, and be vindicated by the positive action of national governments and international organization. States as well as individuals must repudiate racial, religious or other discrimination in violation of those rights.

3. The rights of all peoples, large and small, subject to the good of the organized world community, must be safeguarded within the framework of collective security. The progress of undeveloped, colonial or oppressed peoples toward political responsibility must be the object of international concern.

4. National governments and international organization must respect and guarantee the rights of ethnic, religious and cultural minorities to economic livelihood, to equal opportunity for educational and cultural development, and to political equality.

5. An enduring peace requires the organization of international institutions which will (a) develop a body of international law; (b) guarantee the faithful fulfillment of international obligations and revise them when necessary; (c) assure collective security by drastic limitation and continuing control of armaments, compulsory arbitration and adjudication of controversies, and the use when necessary of adequate sanctions to enforce the law.

6. International economic collaboration to assist all states to provide an adequate standard of living for their citizens must replace the present economic monopoly and exploitation of natural resources by privileged groups and states.

7. Since the harmony and well-being of the world community are intimately bound up with the internal equilibrium and social order of the individual states, steps must be taken to provide for the security of the family, the collaboration of all groups and classes in the interest of the common good, a standard of living adequate for self-development and family life, decent conditions of work, and participation by labor in decisions affecting its welfare.